"Start Your Business with Very Little Money"©
By
Rod Condit

Copyright March, 2009
ISBN: 1442121475
EAN-13: 9781442121478

Start Your Business with Very Little Money

"Start Your Business with Very Little Money"©
By
Rod Condit
P.O. box 412
Placentia, Ca
92871

This Book Is Dedicated To:

The honest, hard working, focused
Individuals who give one hundred percent
Effort to the task at hand, shows up each day
Ready to work, generally a pleasure to be around
And *STILL* struggles to get by financially.

Contents

Start Your Business with Very Little Money

Introduction

I want you to succeed:

- ➤ **Increase your income by a significant amount of money.**
- ➤ **Gain the recognition you deserve for your efforts.**
- ➤ **Have the freedom to be on your own schedule.**
- ➤ **Take control of your financial future.**

Being self employed for most of my adult life, I have helped many people start their own business. All of them had very little money, yet each one had the determination to find a way to begin, survive and ultimately thrive. You can too.

Lack of Money (working capital) is listed as the number one reason why new businesses fail. Most <u>successful</u> self employed people will argue that the following statement is closer to the truth.

To start and have a successful business, you must possess the following, in *this* order of importance:

1. Passion for your chosen profession.
2. Inner drive to overcome every hurdle in your mind and in the world.
3. The self discipline to sacrifice luxuries and comfort, when needed.
4. A customer focused mindset with a positive attitude.
5. Patience to thoroughly research and conduct proper planning.
6. An ability to judge yourself correctly.
7. The willingness to perform hard labor, when required.
8. Money
9. A little luck

Start Your Business with Very Little Money

    This book will give you the tools needed, but the passion, drive and determination has to come from you and only you. If you're currently employed, I suggest starting your new business "on the side". Keep your present job and work part-time at your business until there is enough demand for your products or services. If you plan to lease equipment or store space, at least one year of the required monthly payments should be set aside before attempting to open. Every situation is different and each person has their own risk tolerance and mindset.

    For me, being self employed is richly rewarding. When I work, I am very productive and I make much more money than an employee doing the same job. I schedule work to meet *my* needs as well as the customers' needs. I am responsible for my income and my life. If it is to be, it's up to me. Consider joining me on this journey of self reliance.

CHAPTER ONE

Consider This....

Above All Else, Go With Your Heart

If you <u>already</u> know what you'd like to do for the rest of your life, consider yourself blessed. People who absolutely love their jobs are usually very content. Imagine waking up in the morning and the first thought of the day is: "whoo-hoo! I get to go to work today", Priceless!

Think for a moment what kind of job you have always secretly wished you could do. Now, imagine that people gave you bucketfuls of money and praised you whenever you are doing THAT profession! It's an upward spiral. The more passionate you are about your job, the better you perform; which leads to more demand for your services, which leads to more money and recognition, which leads to more comfort, security and happiness. Up and up it goes. I urge you to pursue whatever it is that you love now, at almost any cost. Jump over the hurdles and go around man made blockades. *Passion is the nuclear reactor that gives you endless energy in life.*

One Way to Find Your Passion in Life

Maybe you have a dream that is not possible at the moment. You think to yourself, "If I was a "fill in your dream job here", my life would be fantastic! I *would* jump out of bed on Monday morning, yelling at the top of my lungs: <u>YES! YES! , I GET TO GO TO WORK TODAY!!!</u>" That idea, dream, passion or hope you have, *has* clues towards your true calling, and *that* is certainly worth exploring. Follow along with me for a short time. The idea here is to clarify your thoughts, to understand what desires drive *your* passion in life. Let's examine a life and see what really makes a person a successful "your dream job":

9

Is it just the "dream job"?
1. You think, talk and are consumed with "your dream job".
2. You know every aspect, theory and rule involving "your dream job".

Or is it something about "your dream job" that most likely drives you?
1. You desire to socialize with other "your dream job" people.
2. You like being known as a "your dream job".
3. You relish the challenge of making a difference in that field. (What difference and how would you go about it?)
4. You focus on "your dream job" and your problems disappear.
5. You get inside benefits and/or information that is not available to the "outside world".

Is it the successful mindset?
1. You posses a determination to be at your best, to reach just a little beyond your capabilities while being involved in "your dream job". You will the impossible to become possible through practice and persistence.
2. You possess the self discipline to pursue your goals even when you *really* don't feel like it at times.
3. You believe in yourself, yet accurately consider other peoples' evaluations.
4. You are a valued member of this world, doing important work.

Is it the results of being successful?
1. You have enough money to take care of your family and pamper yourself in luxury.
2. You are respected for your talents.
3. You achieve fame and notoriety from others in your field and possibly the public.
4. You become more desirable to the opposite sex from your success.

Your answers probably are a mixture of the reasons why you have always dreamed of becoming a "your dream job". If you read back

Start Your Business with Very Little Money
through the list, some aspects are more evident to you than others. We (meaning you) need to further clarify the reasons.

Make list with "your dream job" at the top of a paper; write down every detail, including what kind of clothes you are wearing, of what your "day to day" life would be like doing *that* job. Put a check mark on those activities that appeal to you the most, and form a more accurate picture of what drives your passion. Take some time to consider how you can use your true passions to achieve *those* goals and not necessarily in that particular profession.

Choose a path that is right for *you*, regardless of any fears of failure you may have. We can make excuses why it won't work or we can decide that nothing or no one will stand in our way. Being self employed is a big ego boost in itself. Most likely, you will make more money, but passion is the difference between barely surviving and wildly thriving. Heed this warning from **MY** experience; you are either heading in the right direction or you're not. Your efforts will become easier when you are going with your gut feelings and not your fears.

Think about successful people you know or have seen on television. They are passionate and focused about their profession, being the best that they can be in their life. People are drawn to them. Your passion gives you focus and energy to accomplish your goals without wasting time or effort. Overall, people will do business with you (and will talk about you to their friends and family) because of the positive energy they get from being near you, because you are genuine and sincere about your passion in life. Get to the bottom of what drives you and have the courage to face your fears.

Learning the Right Mindset
It seems that almost everyone is going through hard times. Depressing news is everywhere. Dealing with your own issues of losing your home, your job and your financial stability is hard enough without having to see it happen to your friends, family and acquaintances too. This world is geared towards taking advantage of anyone who is *already* beaten down or has made a mistake. Take your punishment, even if you didn't deserve it, and move on from here. Make a decision today to look

11

toward the future and begin to build YOU back up; mentally first, then financially.

Begin by focusing on the positive to bring a sense of balance and mental health back to your life. Take small steps to take care of yourself <u>first</u> before anyone or anything. This selfish act actually benefits everyone who cares about you. You will have a better sense of well being that will help you be more productive, happy and focused. Some examples are to: build on healthy and desirable relationships, take an online class, practice playing an instrument, learn a new language, go to one day seminars, read informational books and magazines, begin to exercise ... anything that benefits *you* directly in a positive, healthy manner. Soon you will begin to *really* believe in yourself and that *anything* is truly possible.

Second, establish a network of friends and acquaintances by building on genuine connections made with people you meet. Never be desperate, just be a <u>little</u> forward on your approach. You need people and they need you. Why? Friends and associates do small favors for each other that take hardly any effort from the giver, *but* means a great deal to the receiver. It is a give and take relationship, other wise you are using them only for your benefit; or you are being used only for their benefit. That kind of relationship never last long. Be more sociable with; neighbors, friends of friends, strangers while shopping, etc. Drop your guard a little to connect with those outside your usual group of friends and family. Another method is to do volunteer work anywhere there is a need. Think about how easy it is to meet people at work; the same principals apply while volunteering.

Word of mouth is the cheapest (free), most effective form of advertising. Connecting with people who are in related businesses, but do not provide the service or product you offer are the best contacts to make. A few business cards in the right hands can be the key to getting a huge break, especially if you're a casual friend. Be more sociable, even if it feels unnatural at first, it becomes easier with practice.

Third, make an effort to realize what other people are discussing, what you're watching on television, hearing on the radio and reading on the internet. If you're being over loaded with negative information, change the subject, just turn it off, change the channel or skip that internet page. Yes, you should be alert to the news in Washington D.C., your state and area; but don't keep watching and focusing on bad news. It doesn't help, but hurts your state of well being. Focus on what is good, pure, wholesome, healthy and innocent.

Fourth, it is a known fact that people are unable to focus clearly or achieve much of anything when they are being pursued, prosecuted, and under pressure. Know that clearly, now. Make a decision to put your troubles aside when there is nothing you can do about it at that moment. Focus your mind on what you can do to get ahead and *just do it*, not to just get through another day or week. Practice this mindset every single time you begin to dwell on your problems.

Positive self talk is one of the key ingredients you will need to learn and eventually master to become as successful as you want to be. Everyone has moments of doubt. Sometimes those moments can last a long time or a life time when we refuse to muster the courage to overcome hurtful comments and actions made by people who were momentarily (or permanently) thoughtless. Once you get in gear, stay in gear and blow off, ignore and discount any one who speaks and acts from their own insecurities and jealousies.

Truly change your life with imagining what's possible and exert the energy with every fiber of your being to accomplish what your heart desires. Learn to give yourself small rewards for each success. Change your outlook on life, you change your world. *Grab the bull by the balls and hang on for life.*

Plant the Seed
Once you think this through and decide to say to yourself, "I am going to do this", your subconscious mind begins to think and act as if the business already exists. It seems as if every bit of information that could possibly relate to starting that business will catch your attention. Again, think it through, do your homework, do the math and *decide YES or NO.*

Picture in Your Mind if You Will…

Start Your Business with Very Little Money

Visualize what your business will look like, *eventually,* to the very last detail. A clear, precise picture in your mind makes motivation seem almost effortless through difficult times. Day to day decisions become easier and should always point you towards that end goal. You will instinctively prepare for each next step. *Be the man with a plan.*

Take Risks in Small Steps

You took a risk buying this book. After reading the entire book, you will evaluate weather you did, or did not, receive your desired information. By making an effort to take small, calculated risks often, it becomes easier to make wise decisions. Like shooting at a target; with practice you get better and better. Soon, a wrong decision will be evaluated, easily laughed-off and used as a learning experience. You will *know* your decisions are generally wise and fruitful.

Advice is Easy to Get, Take it All

People love to give their opinion and advice. When formulating your ideas, ask as many people as will listen to you about what they think of your plans. The more diverse opinions you get the better. Consider the source of each opinion. This also paints you, (rightly so) as an underdog and people love underdogs! Some acquaintances will root for you and encourage anyone they meet to use your business just to help you get started. Many people will heap good will on you, like you were their first born. Compile all the advice they give you in your head and a common theme or idea or issue will keep popping up. Wisely consider the idea or issue before solidifying plans.

On the other hand, be prepared for some odd reactions. Many will be full of support and will honestly try to give you their best advice and sincerest opinion, which is wonderful. Some will *say* they are sincerely supportive yet, their body language displays something different. Surprisingly, some will even consciously or subconsciously attempt to sabotage your plans. Try not to take it personally.

Mentors

Start Your Business with Very Little Money

Somewhere along the road, you will find a mentor, or they will find you. It just comes naturally. Mentors have been through it already and most likely, have seen just about everything there is to see. Experienced advice is an important tool. To be able to pick up the phone and solve (what you thought was) a major crisis, just by speaking to "someone who's been there", is a huge weight off your shoulders.

Mentors have no ulterior motives. They answer your questions with an attitude of "this is my advice, take it or leave it". Their interest in your business ranges from slightly interested to mildly interested. In reality, they enjoy being appreciated and valued. The good news is; that's all they require for their "payment". They don't necessarily have to be in the same type of business as you, but by simply being a business owner, they are invaluable.

Honesty Pays in So Many Ways

When people know that you deal with them honestly and charge fair prices, they almost refuse to do business with anyone else. They will even wait for you to return from vacation rather than do business with anyone else. They trust you from your personality, attitude and actions. If you suggest an expensive item or repair, they will know that they need it, because you said so. They don't question your integrity or intentions. Most people will not even shop around for another price, because they trust you.

Honesty is not "fake-able". I have watched salesmen and servicemen put on a good show for quite a while until they start answering questions vaguely or with half-truths. Their work ethic is constantly lacking from being in the habit of cutting corners on just about everything from paperwork to performing tasks.

Being consistently honest with your words and your actions takes effort, practice and *patience with yourself*. Soon, it will become as natural as tying your shoes. Being honest means doing what you say you are going to do. Give clear answers to questions that come from uninformed people by explaining in layman's terms the actual facts. Take responsibility for any errors or misunderstandings immediately, regardless of time and cost. Be friendly yet not overly forward. Connect on human terms by showing empathy. The rewards are fruitful with

15

steady work, a clean conscious, great pay and respect from your customers. *Get your customers to swear by you, not at you!*

Creativity Beats $$

Advertising is expensive, especially when you have very limited funds. The most effective advertising (besides word of mouth) for your business isn't always the most expensive. Advertising can be unproductive if you allow someone else to create the ad. They will not have your passion and desire to succeed. You must come up with concepts, ideas and plans to spread the word.

Listen to the advertisers' marketing department, but realize that they are in the business to make as much money off of <u>you</u> as possible, not to necessarily sell your product or service. Many times, they will create a marketing plan for your business directly for YOUR EGO (especially if they sense that you have a big one) instead of what would *really* work.

Create a list of every imaginable way you could promote your business regardless of how wacky they look on paper. Once you have written down every possibility, leave the list alone for a day or two and review it. A light bulb idea may appear over your head while reading through a second time. Consider the idea with a combination of:

A. Gut instincts
B. The least expensive
C. Easiest to start
D. Simplest to maintain.

Imagine spending a large amount of money on an advertisement that didn't even bring in enough customers to pay for itself, before expenses! Even *if* the expensive advertising *does* work; most likely, there will be days, weeks or months before you know if it was a wise investment or not. That can cause some sleepless nights and gut wrenching days.

Now, imagine if the advertising was inexpensive. If it was successful, you would be a brilliant business man, if it fails, so what! <u>No</u>

16

<u>advertising company will give you a guarantee that your ad will work to your expectations.</u> *Don't bet the farm on unknown results, regardless of what the advertising company says.*

It Pays To Treat Everyone the Same

America is becoming a very diverse country. There are people here who come from many different countries, with different customs who speak English as their second language. The accents can be thick and hard to understand with mispronounced words and meanings. Be aware of your own prejudices when dealing with people. Their money is just as good, sometimes better, when you learn that a competitor walked away because of the difficulty to communicate and/or be able to handle different negotiation customs.

People are people. You have 90% of the same hopes as almost every one on this planet. Most people are good and a few are bad; in every race, religion and nationality. Everyone should be given a chance to show their own character, without pre-judgment. They (anyone that's different from you) will usually give the same respect you give them.

Life is a Balance

The excitement of starting a new business can begin to slowly take over your entire life. Exceptions for working late and on weekends can become the normal routine. You will be more productive and happier if you set limits for maximum hours per day and/or days worked in a row. Your loved ones will appreciate it. What is the value of money and success without your family and health? Nothing!

CHAPTER TWO

Basic Business Needs

Get Legal ASAP

Do your best to become legal as soon as possible. There are numerous government agencies that require licenses, permits, fees, taxes, payments etc. The penalties range from none to severe for non compliance. Sometimes, a penalty depends on if you contact them first before they contact (catch) you. Find out the penalties for noncompliance first and then check your own risk tolerance.

Consider the big picture, everybody benefits from you starting your business and making money. You will now provide the community with an *additional* product or service selection. Through your earnings you will purchase needed items that are taxed. Those items provide employment and profit to other companies. When you start to make money, the government will get a percentage of your profits. When you grow enough to need help, you will provide needed jobs that support other families. Before you do any of this, you need to survive when just starting out. *Keep the boat afloat.*

Doing Business As:

If you want to name your company "Amazing" Plumbing Company instead of using your own name, like "John J. Doe" Plumbing Company; you need to file a *fictitious business statement* in order to conduct business. Do an internet or phone book search on your town, county or state for how to file. The fees are usually less than a hundred dollars. Be sure to come up with at least three different names for your business prior to filing, in case your first and second choice names are

18

already being used. Some states have an internet search for names already being used.

Don't use Microsoft Management Company unless your last name is Microsoft, and even then, expect probable legal problems. Most existing companies will vigorously pursue legal action on any new business name (sometimes, years later when they learn about it), that could possibly, in any way, be confused with *their* name or type of business. To avoid a lawsuit, everything must be changed immediately: signs, business cards, invoices, print advertising, brochures, bank account information, etc.

Some Businesses like to name their company with an advertising advantage of being seen in the phone book. Here are two completely different ways:

A. For business directory listing (like The Yellow Pages™), use AAA-1 Termite Company. When a customer looks in the business directory under termite repair, AAA-1 is the first listing they will see.

AND/OR

B.   For a basic phone book listing (residential and business names), use Terry's Termite Company and request your company name be printed in **bold**. Your name will be seen on the same page in the "TER" section. Anyone who turns to a basic phone book looking for a termite repair company will usually find only one listing, Terry's Termite Company.

Typically, the clerk will show you how to do the paper work, and; explain how to publish the new name in a newspaper for a few weeks, to have the document become legal. Once that's been completed, they mail you back a "proof of filing". Take that paperwork to any bank and open a checking account to deposit the money you're soon going to make. A business checking account makes bookkeeping much easier to figure income, expenses, taxes and most importantly, profit!

Mailing Address

Start Your Business with Very Little Money

Once you file a fictitious business name, all the business to business companies flood you with solicitations. A Post office box may be a good idea. This also allows you to not be locked into a fixed location, in case your landlord decides to jack your rent up or the place isn't working for you. A word of caution, I was once burned by a private mail box company who decided to close their doors without notice. I had to scramble for weeks trying to get checks reissued and get a genuine post office mail box afterwards. I never did get that lost mail from them. I suspect they just threw it away. Also, unless you don't mind having your home address published in the newspaper from the fictitious name filing; get a genuine Post Office Box. Be advised that some businesses will *not* accept a check written from a business account with a P.O. Box listed as the only address.

Business Phone Number

Business phone numbers usually cost more than a typical residential telephone line. You could chose to start out using your existing residential phone for your new business. Once a residential number is advertised as a business in the phone book (residential or business services directory), the phone company will automatically switch that number to a business line and begin to bill appropriately. Once a phone number is designated a business line, it can not be changed back to residential billing.

When a business phone account is obtained, the phone company usually offers a better phone number that has repeating digits, for example: the last two digits could be "00". Customers will have an easier time remembering the number. A common practice is to get a business phone number and then forward the phone to a cell when you are not home. Customers have an immediate response for questions or setting up appointments.

Printing Needs

Now that you have a legal business name, a mailing address and a phone number, it is time to bring it all together for the printer. Make time to create some preliminary drawings (regardless of how crude or elementary). Make notes of your desired choices on colors, letter font styles, logo ideas, sign sizes and shapes. The same theme can be used for business cards, invoices, letter heads, vehicle signs etc. A good printer will have a graphic artist onsite to create just about anything. Come with an open mind as the artist should provide many samples and ideas regarding how the final product will appear.

To cut costs, most printers will have pre-made forms for different types of business needs. They print your business information on each pre-printed form. Nebs.com offers just about everything online. Personally, I choose to have a relationship with a local printer. Any type of print ad or brochure is much easier and quicker to put together in mass quantities at a moments notice. He has all my artwork on file, I get personal service and the cost is comparable with online services.

Deciding on Your "Area"

Consider how far you are willing to travel for work. Choosing a pre-determined "area" will establish a mental measuring distance of what is the acceptable travel time and expense is for each individual job. The temptation to go anywhere for any work diminishes quickly after deducting travel costs from the profit. If a situation requires a second trip at no charge, the profit can become less than minimum wages or worse.

A word of caution about giving *free* estimates to distant locations: the further away it is, the less likely you will get the actual work. Most people prefer using a local business. Customers will shop far and wide and will usually hire the guy in their town anyway. They want to verify the local guys' price is competitive. Customers also receive valuable information about the scope and nature of the project by obtaining free estimates. You said "free estimate", so that's what they want.

The exception to this rule is: A) you are a specialized expert in your field and you charge travel time and expenses B) Your service or product is far superior or unique to the competition and is priced accordingly. C) The customer was referred to you through a friend or relative.

Deciding Your Prices

Start Your Business with Very Little Money

The most common mistake for new businesses is charging too much or too little for their products and services. If the prices are *too* low compared to the competition, people will sometimes question the quality of the product or service. Customers will *look* for any reason *why* these prices are so much lower and come to their own conclusions that are either true or conceived.

To build your customer base, charging *very* competitive prices is a way to get the ball rolling *temporarily*. As time goes by, more profitable customers will replace most of the "price sensitive" customers. The closer the business is to being at maximum capacity the more the prices should be increased to match demand.

Another school of thought, especially while you are still working a full time job as your primary income, is to charge the comparable rates of your competition from the beginning. Slowly, you build customers from word of mouth due to your professionalism.

Lease Agreements

The biggest risk to any new business is signing a lease that requires substantial monthly payments. Businesses must pay those expenses even when there is not enough sales to meet the obligation. Most likely, there will be busy and slow months. The business can become a game of constant catch up. Sink behind during the slow months, then; bringing everything current in the busy months. It is best to figure the worst case scenario on how you plan to meet the required payments. Earnings from your current job or savings may be needed for at least a year to meet those obligations. I urge you to practice *extreme caution* when making commitments in the start up phase of the new business.

The more research that is done *prior* to any agreement; the more likely good decisions will be made and less of a risk would be involved. Used or repossessed equipment for just about any type of business can be located and purchased for much less money than new equipment.

Landlords and property management companies *can* negotiate lower rents, regardless of what they say at the first meeting. Keep talking and chisel away at their demands. The more determination displayed, the

22

Start Your Business with Very Little Money

more likely they will come around to meet you in the middle or… they will completely shut you off. There are now plenty of vacancies for space. If they refuse to be reasonable, go somewhere else. Don't be held hostage by agreeing to unrealistic rents or requirements. Remember that you are obligated to pay the rent on the remaining months of the lease, EVEN IF YOU CLOSE YOUR BUSINESS.

City License

If you are conducting a business where no customers or employees will be in your home, a city license should be easy, as long as your city allows it. Bring your new business check book to city hall, fill out the form and pay the fee.

To open a new business at a commercial location, almost all cities require some form of permit, plan, fire inspection and/or fee. Some cities will require a hand drawn diagram of your intended floor plan, your operating hours, what type of business you plan to conduct, how many employees are expected to work there, etc. Some cities will inspect your location prior to allowing electricity to be turned on.

Bookkeeping

Let's face facts here. Some people like (or know how) to do all the required bookkeeping, others do not. However much paperwork you are willing to learn and do, you can find a bookkeeper to do the rest for a very reasonable fee. If you are allergic to paperwork; bank statements, receipts and invoices related to the business can be placed in a large manila envelope and handed to the bookkeeper. Most bookkeepers have a simple system of how they want you to submit your paperwork to them. Interviewing a few different bookkeepers would clearly help you choose which one is right for you. Some are more sympathetic to the paperwork challenged individuals, others expect you to follow along at every twist and turn of a conversation related to bookkeeping. Guess which category I fall into? For all the headaches they save you, they are well worth what they charge.

CPA's

Start Your Business with Very Little Money

Accountants take the bookkeepers paperwork and figure your taxes once every few months (quarterly) or annually. Since so much of your money COULD go towards paying taxes, the accountant easily pays for his services in savings. The accountant also takes time to inform you on upcoming allowable deductions for the next year. Any correspondence from the state or IRS is looked over, explained to you, and answered by him. After you leave the accountants' office the first time, you will realize, *that by listening to his advice*, you are now making more money yet paying less in taxes, than when you were working for someone else! **This is the bottom line reason why the rich get richer and why YOU should be in business for yourself.** This is a major benefit to being self employed.

Sellers Permit

If merchandise is purchased for resale, a license or permit is required in order to collect sales tax for the state. Typically, a small deposit is required based on your expected gross sales. With a sellers permit, any purchases made for later resale are untaxed. The resale permit number and purchases are documented by each wholesaler that does business with you. When the items are sold, you collect the tax and send that money to the state on a monthly or quarterly basis. The bookkeeper can fill out the paperwork and you send a check with the form.

If your business is in the repair industry, you may not need to get a resale license, depending on your state. (Check to be sure, verify!) Here is how it works; state sales tax is paid on all items at the time of initial purchase. When that item is used for a repair, a "flat rate" is charged for both parts and labor to the customer. If items are listed on the bill separated from labor, and you are selling the item for more than what you originally paid, a resale permit is required. Be aware that taxes must be paid by you from any out of state purchases when sales tax hasn't been collected for your state. Again, find out the rules of your state involving sales tax reporting.

Accepting Credit Card Payments

Once you have filed your fictitious business name, many credit card processing companies will be calling to get your business. They will attempt to sell you a credit card processing machine and sign you up for service. Some processing companies charge a monthly fee, <u>AND</u> charge you for each credit card transaction, <u>AND</u> charge you a percentage of each sale on top of that. The percentages and plans vary and can add up. There are *many* processing companies. Your bank may offer a discounted rate and possibly process payments faster. Be sure to compare plans and services prior to agreeing to a contracted time frame. Be aware that you may need decent credit, personal references and your business must be verifiably reputable.

One *credit card* company charges *you* a monthly fee to accept *their* credit card AND will quickly reverse a payment, if the customer requests it for <u>*any* reason</u>. This certain credit card company will not even consider your objections (<u>regardless</u> of your proof of service or sale of merchandise to the customer). *That* credit card company instructs you to locate the customer and demand payment <u>without any assistance from them</u>. **Read the fine print closely** on any papers the credit card companies send directly to you and; you will know immediately which credit card I am referring to.

Typically, payments are deposited into your account after a few days. Unusually large amounts for your type of business (or in the beginning), may take two weeks before the deposit is made to your checking account.

If you have a business that accepts payments at different locations, the credit/ debit card can be imprinted on an old fashioned "knuckle buster" and processed for payment on your home computer. If there is a problem with the card, the customer has to be contacted to arrange for a new payment method. A device is available to plug into your cell phone to "swipe" the card for payment. If you have a laptop with a satellite wireless internet, a "card swiping device" can be plugged into a USB port and the transaction can be completed immediately. If you have a fixed business location, some cash register "point of sale" machines have card swiping capabilities and you choose your desired processing company.

CHAPTER THREE

Advertising and Marketing

These advertising strategies are listed from the least expensive to the most expensive methods. This chapter does not cover every method for every area, as some communities have their own "bulletin board" that is inexpensive yet highly effective.

Word of Mouth

Friends, family, church members, group members and acquaintances will usually give you their business. If you are highly likeable and sociable, they will also get *their* friends and family to call you too.

The most effective word of mouth campaign is to target people in companies that are related to your industry somehow. People often ask employees of businesses that they already know and like for referrals to other good businesses. Be casual about building business relationships with people. No one likes an anxious pusher. Be sociable, easy going and friendly to people who could give you many referrals. Never seem desperate for business, but always be available to service more customers, especially if it is one of their friends or family members. Give them great service and again, be sociable, friendly and easy to get along with. People do business with people they like and are comfortable with, be that type of person.

Start Your Business with Very Little Money
Volunteering and Sponsoring Community Events
Some people are *very* involved with their church, organization, club or cause. This sounds cheesy, but yes, gets more involved. Become an usher at church, sponsor the high school football booster club, whatever you're already into, get more into that. Not only will the members appreciate your good will, they will remember you when they need something you provide. Very successful people, who have money and time, are usually very active in their group. Many times, you can't tell them apart from anyone else there. They dress and talk like everyone else, except that they're wealthy and connected. They know other successful business leaders and, with a word, could get you a tremendous amount of work or a gravy contract. They may just give you a tip about a company looking for exactly what you specialize in. You may not like it, but that's the way it is.

Internet Broadcasting
Place an ad on craigslist.org and other free websites. The ad needs to be reposted every day for craigslist.org. Social networking sites are useful, especially if what you do is "cool".

No Cheap Sign Printing…
Some computer programs offer templates for business cards and signs. The time required to master the program and be able to produce a professional look is not easy, unless you have a serious knack for artwork design. The cost of the ink cartridges of a typical home computer printer doesn't justify the expense compared to the quality and price of a professional sign from a commercial printing company.

…Unless You Are Really Desperate
I have seen home made signs that are advertising a business. It does work. It looks very unprofessional and most likely; people probably expect to pay much less for the service advertised. There is a roofer that lives in my area. He sprays red spray paint through a stencil onto a scrap piece of cardboard and then staples the sign onto a stake. He plants them in fields along busy roads and tapes them to telephone poles at intersections. "ROOFING REPAIRS" CALL (555)555-5555. A ten year old child could make a better sign. Seriously, that's how bad they look!

Start Your Business with Very Little Money

How do I know this works? He has been posting signs in different locations in this area for well over four years now. If he wasn't making any money, he would have stopped a long time ago.

Personalized Neighborhood Letters with Stickers, Magnets

Choose a neighborhood of about 500 homes and write down each physical address. Write by hand each envelope with "neighbor" or "Occupant" with their address. You can purchase a neighborhood mailing list with their names. Mailing list providers have a minimum order policy and can be found on the internet by doing a search. A hand written envelope has more of a personal touch and is more likely to be opened.

Write down everything you could possibly want to say to customers about your business. Introduce yourself as a new business in their area, offer a 10% discount only for your neighborhood. Take a second paper and write down your more focused thoughts, and copy from the first list the best wording and anything that stands out as appealing to your eyes. Take a third paper and rewrite your personalized letter to get the wording closer to perfection. Enclose magnets, business cards, self adhesive stickers. In your letter, ask them to place the magnet on their refrigerator, ask them to put the self adhesive sticker anywhere related to your business, like on the garbage disposal for drain cleaning, or furnace for duct cleaning, or on the back of their television for A/V service, or on their garage door railing for garage door service, you get the idea. Take your personalized letter to an office supply store or a printer to make copies. Paper clip or staple your sticker or magnet to each letter. Use real stamps to mail, not the postmasters stamp.

One mailing to 455 homes in my area <u>provided half of all my customers</u> for many years. I included stickers, a hand written envelope with a typed, personally signed letter. Eventually, I worked for 15% of all the homes in the neighborhood and also provided service to their friends and family outside of the area. Basic advertising usually costs about 10-20% of your gross income to get new customers. The mailer was overwhelmingly successful.

28

Start Your Business with Very Little Money

Personally, a flyer that is left on my screen door never even gets looked at; it goes straight to the trash can. I am irritated that I have to constantly clean these up. As for my mail, well, I am going to get the mail anyway. Any obvious advertisement that I'm not interested in, gets tossed immediately. A hand written letter, even addressed to neighbor, is opened. Anything free like a magnet and stickers are always appreciated and used or given to kids to play with. There are multitudes of shapes for magnets. An internet search will help you find a magnet company that will print your business name, phone and slogan for pennies each. They will customize your magnet for more money. Think about how many homes you have been in that have fun advertising magnets on their refrigerator!

Business Directory Phone Book Advertising

Your advertising dollars need to be spent as efficiently as possible. Some business directory phone books have "designated areas". If your desired service or delivery area straddles two separate phone book coverage areas, it will cost you twice as much to advertise in both books and you will end up turning down some work that is too far to travel in either direction. A phone call to your local business directory listings representative will give you the information. A big ad cost big money. A smaller, more creative, catchy ad would be more effective and cost efficient.

The ONLY business directory that is worth advertising in, is the same company that **also** provides the local phone service to *that* area. The *other* business directory phone books, which do not also provide phone service to that particular area, are a complete waste of money. Check the areas you would like to advertise in, you may be surprised that another phone company provides the local home phone service than the one you expected.

Keep in mind that many phone books are kept and used year after year and a new book sometimes gets tossed in the trash. Wait at least two years before realizing the full potential of your advertisement. You will be paying for other forms of advertisement today, while paying for the phone book ad that will be productive in a year or two.

Start Your Business with Very Little Money

Some phone book representatives are particularly greedy and will hike your advertising rates a hefty percentage every year, even without changes from last year. Many directory sales reps. get a bigger percentage for selling you a bigger ad, some color or enlarging your area. Don't be afraid to negotiate aggressively the first time and don't agree to a massive rate increase later. If they refuse to budge on their prices, make your ad smaller.

Church, organization, club, or *local small company (ask them where the company is headquartered)* directories are personalized to a select group or area and are considered valuable to advertise with and are cost effective.

Business to Business (B2B) Directory Phone Book Advertising

Some communities may not provide this book with all listings in the business services directory. The communities that have the B2B book use this advertising to reach only businesses. Most businesses use both books when attempting to locate a product or service anyway. If you are trying to reach only businesses, I would still advertise in both books, unless the phone company has that particular category listing only in the B2B directory. Remember, who ever provides the phone service for that particular area is the only phone book worth advertising in.

Newspaper and Penny Saver (Bargain Shopper) Advertising

Lately, these two advertising sources are a little expensive compared to the responses. If you are specifically targeting the older, established crowd like senior citizens, advertise in newspapers. Home services ads in newspapers could be run consistently on Thursday through Sunday. Newspapers have their highest readership on those days. Anyone looking to make home repairs will be looking for services on the weekend or right before, when it is on their mind.

If you are specifically targeting bargain shoppers and penny pinchers; advertise in the Penny Saver type of publication. Penny Saver customers will not make you any money worth mentioning the first time you provide service. If you are professional and polite and charge really low prices, they will call you back and refer their friends to your company; which *is* profitable and steady work.

Start Your Business with Very Little Money

Write your advertising in each publication to fit *their* primary readers. Be creative and take time to word the ad to stand out. Look at competitors' ads and unrelated business ads to get ideas. Take a little from each ad you like and change or combine the wording to fit your needs. If you desire, advertise a service or product that is your specialty at a deep discount. The special price is *only* for a basic service or product. Anything extra or upgraded is charged at regular prices. When face to face with a customer that is set on *only* the advertised special, honor it with full customer service and a good attitude. Once a customer has used your service, they are much more likely to call you back for something else, unless you have a sourpuss expression the first time. The publications advertising department can help word your advertisement, but only to encourage more costly wording, and get you to hurry up and finish the ad order. Either publication needs to be run consistently. Some customers may not need your service or product right now, but will remember seeing your ad before in that publication and look through a new issue to find you.

Vehicle Wraps

A vehicle wrap is a magazine quality type of colorful graphics and/ or pictures "skin" that covers your whole vehicle (except the windows needed for driving). This is also important if you have a store front location. The vehicle can be parked close to the street for advertising exposure. Driving around the wrapped vehicle will bring added work for years.

A good rule is: the simpler the better. You may have seen those wraps while driving around. Sometimes you have no idea what they're selling because there's so much wording or too many small pictures, unless you're at a signal light and one is right in front of you. A good graphic artist working for a wrap company can help design a sensible vehicle wrap. They need to know the sizing, and where the hinges, windows and curves are on the vehicle. A good wrap company already has a computer program with every vehicle available. They down load the outline of the vehicle and both you and the graphic artist arrange the pictures and graphics together.

Start Your Business with Very Little Money

To ensure your vehicle wrap is effective and makes sense, test your picture or drawing of your design (or provided by your graphic artist) on your family members. Hold the picture up to your chest and run through your home quickly. Ask them what they think they saw on the picture. *If they guessed at least part of it right, it was designed well!* A great vehicle wrap graphic artist will offer you a few different design choices to take home and consider. Use anything from any design option to bring about your original ideas and eventually, you get exactly what you want.

A vehicle wrap will pay for itself. If you took 10% of all the sales that came *directly* from customers who called or came in because of the vehicle wrap; you should get your money back within a year. After that, you have free advertising for *at least* a few more years before it becomes too faded or worn.

It is important to hire a reputable company to wrap your vehicle. They will be more expensive and take longer. They will also push your meager little job aside whenever one of their national accounts calls or needs work. What do you get for the abuse? You get an efficient, cost effective advertising tool that looks professional and clean that will last for many years without peeling. The professional wrap companies can also provide an anti-graffiti coating for an additional cost. You can wipe the spray paint right off with glass cleaner and a rag.

Radio and Television Advertising

Both radio and television are relatively cheap on a "per commercial" basis. In television, the production costs can get high, even for simple ads. Both T.V. and radio require ads to be run repeatedly to catch the customers' attention. It seems that ads have to be completely fun or totally annoying to be effective. The process can not be done half way. Money for continued airing needs to be set aside until name recognition is established. Radio commercial production costs are sometimes included with the contract purchase of airtime.

Commercials get "stale" after being aired hundreds of times. Continuing to repeat the same commercial will cause people to blank out when they see or hear it, like someone who lives next to train tracks or an airport. After awhile, they don't even acknowledge hearing it. The

Start Your Business with Very Little Money
production costs for new commercials can reach tens of thousands of dollars every few months or less.

If having a commercial is important to you; or you have a unique product or service at: *low, low, unbelievably low prices* and the employees to handle the volume of customers, go for it!

Television Infomercials
An infomercial is a thirty minute airing of a commercial, usually played late night on cable or UHF channels. The production and airtime costs require that anything you sell must cost YOU less than one fifth of the selling price for the item. The production companies suggest this formula as reasonable because the cost of the infomercial can be four fifths of every dollar brought by airing the commercial. A local company can advertise locally to build name recognition as long as there is a substantial mark up of their product or service.

CHAPTER FOUR

Customer Relations

Communicating with the Customer over the Phone

Answer the phone with a smile. There is a difference in your voice and attitude when you smile, even if it's forced. Respond to all questions with honesty and sincerity. Become a source of information for people who call, even if it doesn't benefit you immediately. When they or someone they know needs your service or products, they will remember your good will.

Ask the person for their name before answering detailed questions. If they hesitate to answer or change the subject without answering, be leery about the sincerity of the caller. Introduce yourself again, apologize that you didn't get their name and ask for their name again. If they refuse or ignore your second request for their name, stop the conversation. The caller is not returning your courtesy (red flag), not serious about hiring your company, an information collector for a company trying to sell you something or a sneaky competitor fishing for information. If the caller is not a legitimate customer they may be caught off guard, stumble and give you a fake name. You are giving your valuable time to answer their questions; they should at least return the courtesy of giving you their name.

Start Your Business with Very Little Money
Some companies quote prices over the phone. Others will not quote any prices, preferring to see the work in person. This type of company usually has a "trip charge" fee that they collect just to come to the customers' house. Some companies quote the lowest, rosiest scenario prices over the phone; and point out to the customer after arriving, every reason as to why the price is double or triple the phone estimate. Both strategies work, as people will usually go ahead and give the work to the company that is already there.

Discount seekers over the phone are tough to deal with in person. If you really need the work and take the bait, expect the job to be much, much worse than they described over the phone. Being cheap, they will attempt to hold you to your phone estimate. It is better to explain multiple exceptions of "what if's" over the phone before driving over to their house. Sometimes it is better to walk away with nothing from a questionable customer than to risk working multiple hours for minimum wages and fight for your pay if something goes wrong.

Appointment Setting for a Sales Meeting
When scheduling an appointment over the phone, ask if all the decision makers will be there. For example: when speaking to a man, ask him up front if his wife will want to be there to help make a decision, and vice versa. If you need to reschedule for an evening or a weekend to be able to have both of them there at the same time. If there is a spouse, they might verbally trash everything that was discussed without their presence. It is better to explain everything to their face and answer questions on the spot. Imagine driving 30 minutes to a customers house, spending an hour discussing their needs and spend another 30 minutes driving home using your gas money and time, only to be asked to come over and explain everything again when their spouse is present. Shouldn't you ask (almost demand) the customer for the courtesy of having all decision makers present at the first appointment?

Ask for alternate phone numbers while setting the appointment. There is always a chance of being delayed on another project and wanting to notify the customer as soon as possible if you are going to be late or unable to make the appointment that day. Getting alternate phone numbers also makes collecting the final payment easier when you've completed the job.

Start Your Business with Very Little Money

Always call ahead, when you are on your way, to confirm the appointment. Making phone contact before you get there demonstrates courtesy to the customer and also: a phone call encourages the customer to start thinking about the project; the questions they want to ask and what they want to accomplish during the appointment.

At the Door

On the drive to the appointment, YOU should be thinking about what information you received over the phone and what the customer might need. In the back of your mind you should be preparing yourself to be at your best. Arrive at the door neat, organized, alert and calm. Ring the door bell and immediately knock if you couldn't hear the bell ring. Step a few feet away and turn your back to the door and look at their plants or something. Some people like to sneak a peek through the curtains or door peep hole when they hear the door bell and do not want to be caught doing so. Have a card ready in your right hand.

When the customer opens the door; smile introduce yourself and hand them your card. Some people are germ phobic and do not like to shake hands, the card in your right hand helps alleviate the need to shake hands. If they extend their hand for you to shake, a firm two pump shake while maintaining eye to eye contact and saying something like "nice to meet you" is probably best.

Stand in the entry way and maybe even take a small step backwards once inside to allow them to guide you to where they would like to discuss the business. Some people will just stand there and stare at you, if so take charge. Ask them to show you the area that needs work. Go there and inspect the situation with them, make mental or written notes. Ask them what the dislike most about the area as it is now.

Desired seating Arrangement

When arriving at the kitchen table or living room couch, attempt to sit directly across from both of them. It is easier to show both of them samples and read the contract at the same time. Maintain eye contact as much as possible and note the body language of each of them for clues about moods and anxieties. You can immediately stop and probe for questions that they may want answered now. This is not a trick. This is excellent customer service skills by being attentive to their needs. Whatever their concerns are, focus on the issue quickly. Repeat back to the customer what you perceive the issue to be. Once the issue is clear and established, be straight forward with your answer. Do not white wash the matter or answer with half truths. You will quickly gain their respect and get the approval quicker; or be leaving sooner without wasting every ones time.

Closing the Sale

When you have explained everything and the customer(s) have apparently finished asking questions, assume the sale. While they sit quietly, finish writing the paper work, inform them of your intended start date, hand them the contract to look over with a pen for them to use to sign the contract. If they aren't ready to sign the contract, they will tell you, otherwise assume they are ready to go ahead.

Personality Types of Some Customers

I have listed some types of personalities and how to communicate with them effectively. Most customers will display *only slight tendencies* of any type of behavior listed here.

Manager/ Director

An efficient, professional type of person who wants the short answer to any question they ask. The basic, overall answer will allow them to get more clarification with the next question or move on to the next subject, their choice. If he probes the same subject again, begin to give him exact answers to his questions. After the first few questions, you should be able to gage how he wants his answers from you. Be organized and ready to hand them any paperwork, sample or brochure immediately. When he's finished grilling you, place the paperwork immediately with a ready clicked pen in front of him and wait, without saying a word or moving a muscle, until he signs or speaks to you. Do not interrupt his thinking process, just wait.

The Educated Person

Start Your Business with Very Little Money

A highly educated person, such as a teacher or engineer is mainly focused on comparing products, services, cleaning instructions and warranties. Expect to spend extra time providing the information. This type of person is also very "price" conscience but will never admit it. Remind yourself to speak up every time there is a change in options that affect the price. This person will decide who will get his business after exploring all the options and possibilities.

People Pleaser

A people pleaser is hard to deal with sometimes. They are more interested in not offending you than telling you the truth about what they really want. In order to not waste your or their time going over parts of the job or materials that they have no interest, ask, ask and ask questions. Nail their interests down by asking specific questions. Get creative on how you pull information out of them. Otherwise, they will be too polite to tell you themselves. Look for any slight changes in body language or eye contact. If everything is not the way they wanted it, you will never know without probing. When the contract is in front of them ready to be signed, they might say, "I am not ready to sign it right now".

Stone Faced Walls

They speak in a serious monotone voice. They display no emotion or unnecessary changes in eye contact or body language. They ask specific questions like an ex-CIA agent without the bare bulb spotlight in your eyes. Try to remain calm and pleasant. Match their tone and posture while focusing on the task at hand. Once they have come to a conclusion whether to go ahead with the work with you or not, their mood instantly changes. You find out if it's time to leave or sign the paperwork. Either way, they become much, much nicer. Funny type of person (not the ha, ha type). *Don't even think about stretching the truth while under interrogation.*

Depressed Drone

Someone suffering depression is no laughing matter. This type of person may or may not be depressed but appears to be in every way: listless, uncaring and slightly irritated with everyone and everything including you. By being somewhat cheerful and uplifting, you can sometimes bring them out of it, if only for a few moments. Maybe, just enough for you to get them to sign the paperwork so you can go ahead and get to work on their service request. Some days, we all get mired in the muck of life, some of us stay in the muck for a long, long time.

CHAPTER FIVE

Customers to Avoid

Customers are people too and a few people are ethically challenged. The more solid of an individual you are, the more respect they will give you. The more "poo-poo" you take, the more they will push you to bend; some unhealthy people will want to bend you until you're broke and broken. To add salt to your wounds, they begin to start treating you with less and less respect along the way. The reason for this chapter is to warn you of some of the traps set for good natured souls. Be aware and alert when dealing with the following situations and people.

The Lawsuit Happy Customer

A customer who continues to speak negatively about another business is a red flag. They will speak in great detail how this certain business performed terrible work and how they were forced to take them to court over the matter and won a judgment against that company. Another words, they refuse to let the matter go. I understand that being treated unfairly causes wounds, (believe me!) but they won already! Shouldn't they let the matter go as one bad business?

In my experience dealing with this type of person is, this is a veiled threat to you. Anything and anyone can be the cause of their being "mistreated", they're just unhappy individuals. If any part of your job is unsatisfactory in their eyes, even if it is right, you may be in court too.

Write out everything to the smallest detail and discuss the matter clearly. Listen for any twisting of your words when they are replying to you, where there could be any misunderstanding. If so, repeat the whole discussion again to clarify the issue, don't let them play dumb for convenience sake. You must take lots of pictures before and afterwards. Be sure they see you take them; it will discourage certain acts of sabotage to your workmanship if it goes to court.

Manipulators

You will meet a manipulator, as they are the most common type of customer you should avoid. Manipulators try to get you to do something that is not in your best interest. They attempt to get you to "tell me what I want to hear". When you find yourself answering the same questions posed to you slightly different each time, your brain should begin flashing a big red light. They are attempting to grind you down. They want something for free, want you to do something slightly (or major) illegal, they want you to do something that you are not experienced in or do not have the proper equipment to do. If you do get persuaded, expect to pay the consequences if anything ever goes wrong. Sometimes things go wrong years later and he still has the receipt to prove you did the work, leaving you in a whole mess of trouble with the law or a lawsuit. Practice that "you are pushing me" crazy eyed look when they continue to try to manipulate you. He will stop trying or ask you to leave, either way, you win.

Price Grinders

Anybody, including friends, family, neighbors and acquaintances that pressure you to perform work for free or at a huge discount, will be the hardest customer you will ever have to encounter. Nothing to them will be acceptable or right. Sometimes the more you give away, the less respect you get; and they begin to find your work and you personally, unprofessional. They should be nicer, not meaner, but so it is! Be firm on your bottom line price (unless it's your mom). They will give you more respect, be easier to please and be happier with your products or service.

Start Your Business with Very Little Money
Don't believe me? Try this out a couple of times and find out for yourself.

Short Cut Seekers

The situation can change unexpectedly during any job. It is impossible to predict all that could go wrong without giving the customer a twenty page, job specific disclaimer on "what if's". This is impractical for most types of service work. When an incident occurs or something in their house breaks next to where you are working; you must stop, evaluate the problem and notify the homeowner with the available options. If you are capable of performing the necessary repairs, write up a "change order" or another contract for the additional work. Most people will approve the common sense approach for remedying the situation.

The problems occur when the homeowner refuses to pay you or anybody to repair the damaged items. Sometimes they ask you to cover it up and keep working. This leaves you in a sticky liability issue for a future lawsuit, if the problem causes future damage or is discovered later by a new homeowner, they will go after you. It is also very illegal. Sometimes a homeowner will ask you to do an illegal repair, or is refusing to pay you for your work unless it is fixed. If you are persuaded to make a repair that is a band aid approach; sometimes the band aid falls off while you are still working, leaving the whole job a complete mess. The homeowner will then expect you to fix everything on your time and expense, even when he asked for a shoddy repair, even though you had nothing to do with the damages. REMEMBER, YOU TOUCH IT, YOU OWN IT. Refuse to do shoddy repairs, even if you have to walk away. Many times, they will stop you before you leave and agree to the common sense repair.

If they refuse to fix it right and you just know it's not going to be okay:
  a)   Explain that you are ethically unable to repair it that way.
  b)   Unless they agree to the legal repair, you are unable to finish that section.
  c)   If someone else makes the repair, it must be done right before you restart work.

Start Your Business with Very Little Money

Ten Percent of Your Customers Will Cause Ninety Percent of All Your Headaches

I would like to suggest that you freely turn down work from people who are going to be a problem, (as soon as you can afford it). Problem customers can drain you of your enthusiasm and positive energy. You are your own boss. Not being afraid to turn down work is liberating. Turning down some customers will sometimes drive them crazy. People want what they can't have. Many will almost beg you, or give you the job and the additional pay (requirement to deal with difficult customers) you wanted in the first place. Be careful of what you wish for. Sometimes, even the additional pay isn't worth the added headaches and misery. You are the boss of your company, you choose!

Major Accounts

Any customer that provides 50% or more of your income can easily turn into a nightmare. Companies that give small businesses big contracts sometimes have their own lawyers or legal department draw up contracts that are not in your favor. Allowing small changes in a contract for the agreed upon work may turn out to be a money losing proposition. Horror stories are heard about having to redo the work over and over, at a tremendous cost because of a phrase like: "work must be completed to our satisfaction". It doesn't matter if the work was done professionally the first time, it matters that they are happy, which is subjective (meaning *their* opinion, rather than the facts).

Purchasing or leasing equipment to service a major account properly can leave you worse off than when you started. If anything happens to cause you to lose the customer or substantially reduce your profit, you are stuck making payments with less income. What could happen?

1) They figure out that they can do the work cheaper themselves by hiring their own employee and/ or purchasing their own equipment.
2) They begin to demand steeper discounts and/ or more service because of the volume they are giving you, making the job unprofitable.
3) A management change can sometimes eliminate existing vendors and bring in their own friends and/ or familiar vendors.

4) You, or your employee(s) looked at "Ruthie the receptionist" wrong once, (or anything along those lines), and she begins a successful vendetta to get you removed.

Be prepared for any major changes at a moments notice. Consider hiring and training an employee; let him know his job depends on keeping the account happy and well serviced. Do not allow yourself to neglect building other customers. Always have an emergency nest egg to get you through an unexpected loss of income. *Be careful of what you wish for, it may come true.*

CHAPTER SIX

Before You Quit Your Old Job

Don't Burn Your Boss

Let's face it; a few bosses are just bad! There are some supervisors who are decent, respectful and kind people. If you have a civil boss; be set in your mind to keep yourself in check, regardless of how he treats you the final day(s) before you go out the door. Do not take anything from that company. If he is especially difficult, other employees (and maybe customers) will notice how you handled the situation in a respectful manner. When the time comes around for you to hire your own employees, they may come knocking on your door. Some employees may secretly refer work to you in order to make things right for their bosses' bad behavior.

Training

While you are preparing to start your own business, volunteer for more responsibility at your current job. Some employers will take advantage of any initiative you show and begin to start dumping a lot of extra work on you. Count it as earning your way to your own show. You will gain valuable experience in different parts of the business. If you make mistakes, he will guide you, and; his company pays for your failures, not you. Soon, the boss may begin to give you his work too.

43

Start Your Business with Very Little Money

Even better! When you are finally on your own, instead of learning how to juggle daily operations of your business, you can focus on gaining customers. It will also make leaving easier if they give you a meager raise for all your extra efforts.

Trying Out Your Ideas

By sticking around and showing the initiative to learn the business, your suggestions for minor changes are more likely to be heard. This is *their* company, if they refuse, let it go. If they eventually allow you to try, take the initiative to implement the ideas, take charge and follow through to see for yourself how the idea(s) work out. Keep tweaking the ideas to make them successful, or let the unworkable ones go if they continue to fail. However it turns out; good or bad, it's still their company. They will reap the rewards of your successful efforts and pay the costs for the losses. This gives you practice on making "high value decisions" while building confidence for your own operations. Never give away or experiment your "big" ideas while there, the ones that will make your company super successful, just some of the smaller ones. They could try to claim it as company intellectual property, and possibly sue you, since you were working there at the time.

Learning about Suppliers and Business Contacts

Find out who your bosses suppliers and business contacts are will help you find your own. Avoid the mistake of speaking openly of your plans to his contacts; they will inevitably tell him about your future plans. If possible, talk to representatives in a casual manner about the industry, trends and new products being offered. Do not speak to him there, on your bosses time and place, about your own plans. Get a card, if you can do it discretely. If you are asked point blank by your boss, "are you trying to start your own business?" be prepared to be fired immediately, or taken under his wing and *really* get trained. Hopefully, you are opening your business in another area; or are specializing in a type of product or service that your current employer is not interested in pursuing. Every boss is different, use your own judgment.

Managing Employees

Start Your Business with Very Little Money

At some point in the future, you may want or need to hire employees. Managing employees is no simple task, especially when you were a co-worker. And most especially if some dum-dum has been there much longer than you, but never has his act together or showed initiative to be the boss. Gaining experience at being in charge will not make you popular, but will absolutely pay off later. Learning now avoids very expensive legal problems that could come from your own employees. Casually talk to your boss and/or the human resources department manager about potential problems with employees. You will get a major eye opener. Even if you hire someone with impeccable morals and a wonderful reputation, the game can change overnight. Simple steps taken along the way is cheap insurance for potential problems in the future. Put EVERYTHING in writing, have witnesses, document every disciplinary discussion no matter how minor in their employee file. Usually, a good person is a good employee. Be prepared to screen before hiring and fire immediately the ones who don't work out.

Referrals from Your Old Boss

Your boss or former coworkers may refer jobs to you that are unprofitable, too far or are problem customers. Thank the person for the referral! At least the ball is rolling! You can turn those jobs into highly profitable customers by giving your best customer service. Problem customers have a knack for "swearing at you" or "swearing by you". This means, you should overlook their rude behavior and tense attitude and focus on their needs by being extra patient and understanding. Be sure they are overly happy and joyous, <u>even at a loss on the first encounter</u>, when you leave. They will tell everyone they know, weather asked or not, about you and your company. You just earned a die hard advocate who will pay your prices and never use any other company again. They will treat you with respect, because "you understand the *right way* (their way) to do things".

Obtaining His Outdated Equipment

The former boss may notice the look of determination in your eyes and be willing to sell you his outdated equipment. It makes the world of difference and is suitable for your needs. He gets to clear up some space and get some cash. He may even be willing to sell you some inventory, related to your specialization, that's been on his shelves for

Start Your Business with Very Little Money

years. If you're desperate, ask to make payments. Go with your gut feeling. If you think he's asking too much or something doesn't feel right, take some time to look around for other people or companies that are selling equipment that may be less expensive or better suited to your needs.

CHAPTER SEVEN

Business Ideas

This last chapter is dedicated with information on many businesses that can be started with limited funds. Look through all of them for ideas and suggestions. There are many more businesses that can be started with very little money that are not listed here. Hopefully, this chapter will help guide you in formulating your own plans, ideas and marketing strategies. Most of these businesses can be started part-time.

Be fair, if you become an employee just to get trained in a trade or skill, give that employer his moneys' worth by staying awhile and possibly help him increase his sales and/or profit with some of your ideas and efforts. Remember that you will be in his shoes soon enough and what goes around, comes around.

Each listing is broken down into this format.

SN: Strengths and/or skills needed to be successful.

W: What is this business? I give an explanation of what the business involves.

Start Your Business with Very Little Money

HB: How to begin. I describe one or two ways to start this business.

P: Prices usually charged from this type of business or a pricing strategy.

OPE: Out of pocket start up expenses, depending on your ability to find deals.

MI: Marketing ideas and extra money to be made in this business by being creative.

Advertising Mailer

SN: (Strengths needed): Sales experience, organizational skills, networking skills.

W: (What is this business?) Solicit businesses to advertise a coupon with your mailer. Group these coupons together and mail them to a select group of residents. A coupon mailer has various offers from many different kinds of businesses. Restaurants, auto repair companies, dentists, pharmacies, contractors, etc. use coupons to generate sales. The businesses want to offer a discount to bring in new customers or to generate more sales through up selling services and products, once people come in to take advantage of the coupon.

HB: (How do I begin?) Use the competitions coupons as a starting point and adjust the sizing, color or type of coupon to fit your style and taste; what you think will sell. A Graphic Artist will design several different styles for your own coupons to show prospective customers and to get estimates from printers. The graphic artist will be designing each new coupon for each new customer you sign up. You will present the coupon to the new customer for their review and acceptance and receive payment.

Printers, consult with several in your area to estimate costs and the required time to produce the coupons and envelopes. Get pricing for various quantities and at what levels each price break is achieved. Due to the steep discounts your printer will be offering on mass quantities, consider offering the first coupon for free (or deeply discounted) to a potential customer (if there is a strong probability they will give you future business).

A Mailing List Company will provide demographics and sell you the names and addresses (that your printer will put on each envelope). Some printers offer this service too. The demographics (average age, income, marital and homeowner status) will be used to show your potential clients what kind of customers will receive the coupon. The demographics will help you decide *who* and *how many* will receive your mailer and to *what area* the coupons will be mailed. Select an area that has an above average income and sized reasonably large enough to reach enough homes to make advertising with your mailer effective.

The U.S. Postal Service provides a postage permit. All that is required is to fill out a form and pay a fee at the "bulk mailing facility". The postage charge per piece of mail is surprisingly low compared to the standard rates. They issue you a permit number that is printed on each envelope. Check the rates carefully for sizing and weights at each level. The mailer needs to have the maximum amount of coupons for each level of postage rate based on weight. A thick, full envelope will, more likely, be opened and used by the customers.

Decide on a frequency of each mailing (weekly, biweekly or monthly) Give yourself a reasonable time frame on the first mailing to acquire enough coupons. Set a deadline for when the coupons will be mailed and the cutoff date to allow time for printing and mailing. A deadline date will allow customers to set a time frame for how long a coupon is valid. Preferably, coupons expire before or at the next mailing. Every mailing, a few businesses may opt out. But, by constantly selling the coupons to prospective customers, the repeat customers could continue to pay their initial price and the newer customers will pay an increased rate and be more profitable, (due to your demonstrated success of the mailer).

P: (Pricing): your coupon will take practice on what potential advertisers are willing to pay compared to the actual cost of producing the mailer. Find out what any competitors are charging for a similar area, even better if they are far away. Find your "break even" point for how many coupons you must have in a mailer to cover your costs. Add together Printing, postage, mailing list, transportation expense to travel to each business,

Start Your Business with Very Little Money

etc Always be sure to collect payment in full when the customer sees and approves their new coupon. Your printing and postage fees will need to be paid prior to the mailing date.

OPE: (Out of pocket start up expenses): A Graphic artist time to design sample coupons and your travel expenses to sell coupons. Once you have enough coupons to mail, payments received from the businesses should cover the remaining expenses.

MI: (marketing idea): Have some interesting information about your community, both on the outside of the envelope and a flyer type inside. Missing children, information on coming events, fairs, school sports scorecards and awards, humor, spotlight on a local resident, etc. Make up some flyers and envelope concepts and get opinions! The information should be focused specifically to the local community.

Apartment Refurbishing/ Maintenance Service

W: When apartments become vacant, they usually need some repairs, painting and cleaning. Apartment maintenance includes repairing a little of everything: plumbing, electrical, blinds, flooring, holes in the wall, door repair and replacement, etc. Many apartment owners are just investors that are already busy and prefer to outsource the maintenance and repairs.

SN: Handyman skills required. Can begin by offering simple repairs to plumbing or electrical or drywall, whatever skills you already possess and learn the rest as you go.

HB: Work for an existing apartment or motel as a handyman trainee. Depending on how quickly you can learn, stay for at least 6 months to see and learn to repair a variety of fixtures and materials. Advertise with a publication that offers apartment real estate for sale, or is focused on apartment owners. Do an internet search or call a commercial real estate office for the name of local publications.

P: Easily charge $25-35 an hour plus materials. It would be wise, after gaining some experience to have a "menu" sheet for quoting flat rate prices on every repair you can think of, as investors and owners want a pre- determined fixed cost.

OPE: You should already have the basic tools to complete most jobs. Advertising if required is the only other cost needed to get started.

MI: Pass out cards to every apartment and motel you can find in your area. Repeat the process once a month to the same apartments and motels. Be in neat clothing and well groomed. Maintenance work sometimes gets you in the habit of wearing stained clothing, since you don't want to ruin your good clothes. Hand out cards only in good clothes and purchase used uniforms from good will for only a few dollars.

Appliance Repair, Home Service

SN: Mechanically inclined, work well with your hands, not afraid to get a little dirty. Must be willing to learn the different types of appliance manufacturers repair manuals and parts systems.

W: Repair dish washers, microwave ovens, stoves, washing machines, clothes dryers, refrigerators and freezers (with experience in refrigeration)., furnaces and even water heaters (with experience).

HB: Either become employed at a current appliance repair company, (hopefully away from the area you plan to conduct business) and learn everything you can while there, or; find and buy every repair manual on every appliance possible at used technical book stores and manufacturers websites and practice with trashed appliances until you are comfortable doing repairs. The biggest concern is finding what the commonly needed items are to carry in your truck or van. Parts can be found from equipment manufacturers and an appliance parts search on the internet and/or a local business to business phone book. Advertise in the Penny saver, phone book, and neighborhood a flyer with self affixed stickers stapled to each flyer for customers to place on their appliances. A coupon mailer will work as well with consistent advertising.

P: Be extremely cheap for landlords. Count it as your bread and butter just to keep you afloat until you build up enough residential customers for some real profits. Charge an hourly rate based on your competitors prices or charge a flat rate for each separate repair.

Start Your Business with Very Little Money

OPE: Purchasing the needed manuals of common appliance manufacturers, basic tools and some stock inventory to complete repairs on the same trip.

MI: Contact landlords of small and medium sized apartment complexes and motels. Most large apartment complexes will have their own full time maintenance men doing their repairs. Many smaller landlords are quite capable of doing their own repairs but are too busy with their day jobs.

Aquarium Service and Selling Exotic Fish

W: Many homes and businesses have large aquariums. Usually, the fish are exotic, unique and colorful. Aquariums need monthly service to maintain cleanliness and to keep the fish healthy. By selling the fish also, aquarium owners can purchase and have you introduce the new species to his aquarium at the same time you come in for service.

SN: Must have or gain experience from a pet store that sells exotic fish. There's a lot to keeping fish healthy. You must know which kinds are natural enemies and predators to each other. Also, learn or know about salt water systems.

HB: As stated before, you must gain experience prior to offering your services. Acquire used aquarium tanks and have a temperature controlled room to hold and raise your exotic fish. After working for a pet store that sells exotic fish, you will know what equipment, chemicals and parts to carry to be completely efficient. There isn't much you need to start, except customers.

Advertise in the Business services directory and the B2B phone books. Ask your pet store manager if he will allow you to hand out business cards to pet store customers for your services, which you will do after working hours. Every time a customer comes in to purchase or look at exotic fish, probe them about what kind of tank they have at home and ask if they have the service with another company. Find other pet stores that sell exotic fish and ask if you can leave some business cards on a bulletin board. If you are persistent, they will begin to

Start Your Business with Very Little Money
remember you. If one of your competitors is charging too much, you can provide some healthy competition.

While purchasing exotic fish to resell, build a catalog to show customers when servicing their tanks. I suggest a binder with clear insert sheets. Have 8"x 11" color pictures with the price marked clearly on each picture. Thumbing through it will be easy for anyone without having to ask you about each price.

P: $75-125.for each visit, depending on the size of the tank and time required to complete your work.

OPE: Less than $300 for all the equipment, chemicals and spare parts you need. Used fish tanks can be found for $10 to $100.

MI: Make a couple of trips to the fanciest restaurant and building lobbies in every area around your home. Going into the lobby is perfectly acceptable for anyone to do without any hassles. Every time you find an aquarium or fish pond in a fancy restaurant and office building, write the address down and make a note of who is the building property management company. There should be an office on site. For restaurants, ask to see the manager or assistant manager and speak to them about your services. Send them a letter detailing *your* price for your service to *their* system; include magnets, stickers and business cards. You never know when a company decides to change services and give you a try.

Audio/ Visual Systems Specialist
W: More and more homes and businesses have: televisions, DVD players, sound systems, video game boxes and security video equipment. There is a lot of wiring and synchronizing needed to tie all that equipment together. Almost every bar, restaurant and business with a lobby have some audio and video equipment. Someone has to repair and install everything.

SN: Must have experience in audio and video connections. There are very few companies that provide this service. Attempt to get hired to gain more experience, even if it is a long drive from your home.

HB: If you already know every aspect of connecting televisions to

Start Your Business with Very Little Money

computers and sound systems, pass out cards to bars and restaurants to start. There usually is some time between when you start and when your advertisement appears in the business services directory. To reach upscale homes, find a home services magazine specializing in that kind of market. You are just starting out; purchase the smallest advertising space possible. This is a specialized service so your ad will be seen by people who need your service.

P: $60-90 an hour is reasonable.

OPE: Used testing equipment for audio/visual systems, $500-$1000.

MI: Send a letter with your business cards and magnets to every commercial and luxury homes contractor you can find. Be prepared to travel. They will offer you a chance to bid on new projects and major remodel jobs. Be careful and recheck your numbers repeatedly for accuracy, they will hold you to those figures!

Automobile Detailing

SN: Must love cars and have a personality that includes an extraordinary attention to detail.

W: Some people can afford to have their cars look perfect at all times regardless of the current economy. Some companies desire to project an image that includes their fleet of cars, busses, trucks and/or vans to be immaculate at all times. Small used car companies purchase repossessed and trade in vehicles that need detailing and paint touch-ups prior to resale.

The biggest users of an auto detailer are upscale professional business centers with large parking lots. The owner or management company of the business center(s) is contacted for approval to wash and detail vehicles for tenant companies and their employees working at the business park. A general liability insurance policy is purchased by you to cover the owner of the business center in case any legal issues arise from washing and detailing cars on their property. After receiving some type of commitment or sincere interest from the separate companies at the business center, a schedule is set up to come once a week (or more) to wash and detail all the vehicles that tenants and employees bring to you in the parking lot. Almost every day, work will be in one to four separate locations, depending on the established schedule or phoned in requests.

HB: Get training from a current auto detailer (there is a high turnover of employees due to the constant work requirement of meticulous attention to detail, so getting hired should be easy).There are specialty cleaning products that are super effective as well as many tricks to being fast and efficient in the trade. Wholesalers, who sell auto care products, may provide you with the needed instructions for how to use them.

This is not a recession proof business, but there are some among us who will always have the extra cash to spend. It would be wise to maintain, and *constantly improve*, your reputation by performing absolutely perfect detailing every single time, regardless of how much money you are paid. If a customer appears dissatisfied and you can not make it right for any reason, **regardless of who's at fault**, refuse to accept payment. Once you have established your reputation, elite businesses and clients will be searching you out.

P: A standard detailing job costs about $200 and takes three to five hours. An average day after building your customer base, should net $400 to $500 per day.

OPE: A power washer with some kind of water tank is required as some detail and wash jobs are nowhere near a water supply, cleaning supplies, rags and a buffer.

MI: Go where the rich and successful congregate. Make a deal with golf club managers and restaurant valets to pass out your card in exchange for free detailing on their own vehicles. Put on your card "Auto Detailing: it's perfect or it's free, no excuses!" and honor that slogan when necessary!

Auto Glass Replacement Service
W: Broken windows are typically replaced at the customers' home or work. They call and give you their make, model and year of car and which window is broken. You give them a price over the phone. If they approve the work, you order and pick up at the local auto glass

distribution warehouse and go to where the customer is to install the glass.

SN: Experience is a must. Find a job working for a distant competitor. You must have at least a mini truck.

HB: After learning the trade, call all the major insurance companies to start the paperwork to become a contractor. Do an internet search for auto glass distribution warehouses for your area. After showing them your new business license for auto glass replacement service, they will give you a price book or a password to look up the retail or wholesale prices for any make and model available, so you can quickly quote prices over the phone. Set a standard mark-up price. If the windshield cost you $200, and your standard markup with labor is 165%, you can quickly do the math with a calculator to figure out the quote: $330. Working for a distant competitor will help you find where the place is for your area. Place an ad in the business services directory and pass out cards to all the auto body and mechanics shops in your desired area.

P: Ask insurance companies what they are paying "to see if you can give them a much better deal". Be super competitive when just starting out and give each customer first rate service.

OPE: Basic window installation tools are about $250 and build a window rack on the back of your truck $100. If you work for cash customers, you need the money to pay for just a couple of windshields at a time. When you begin working for insurance companies, auto body shops and mechanics, expect to be paid up to a month later. You will need to build up some working capital and/ or establish credit with the glass distributor.

MI: Contact companies with a fleet of the same type of cars, pickups or trucks. Note the make and model and find the price of a typical installation. Contact the fleet manager in person and with a letter explaining your new business and that you are offering the cut rate price for his vehicles.

Baker of Pastries, Cakes, Pies and Treats

SN: Baking experience in large quantities with delicious recipes. Possess the organizational skills to maintain the needed ingredients and to meet orders.

W: Sell pastries to businesses that will resell them to their customers.

HB: Decide on your list of specialized products and prices and print them on a menu type of flyer. Connect with catering companies, nursing homes, restaurants, cafeterias, party planners and retail stores to resell your products. Most cities and counties require a health department permit. Most likely, in your city there is a pizza parlor or restaurant that does not operate 24 hours a day, probably several. Get an agreement with an existing business to use their kitchen after hours. In tough times such as these, it is easier to find a willing restaurant or pizza parlor who wants to gain extra income with almost no extra effort. Offer to pay his gas and electric bill over his normal usage and a percentage of your gross sales (5 to10%). Each day, write down the numbers of both the gas and electric meters when you get there and when you leave. Keep the noted meter readings in plain sight for the owner to verify daily. In return, you get a health department certified kitchen and the capacity to produce mass quantities of product. Get an agreement to store your cooking utensils and ingredients in an out of the way location.

To get an agreement with an existing business will take determination and persistence. Keep returning with a card in hand to the business to show your honest intention of making it work for both of you.

OPE: Purchasing the needed baking ingredients and acquiring the needed kitchen utensils from a used restaurant supply/ auction house.

MI: Drop off business cards, a flyer, and an order form with a fax number with a different sample every week to every possible customer until they order from you or won't let you in the door. They will begin to look forward to seeing you! Guilt them into ordering, who could refuse?

Bathtub Refinishing

W: After years of use, old bathtubs look unsanitary and worn out. People hire refinishers to acid wash the tubs and put a new coat of special paint

Start Your Business with Very Little Money

that is designed just for refinishing tubs. Refinishers also patch holes in fiberglass tubs and fill in chips in other types of tubs and tile using bondo and fiberglass. Besides refinishing tubs, there is plenty of demand from the same customers to refinish cultured marble, counter tops (amazing new granite and marble types of paints!) sinks, wall and shower tiles and appliances (refrigerators, stoves and microwave ovens).

SN: Attention to detail, customer relations, must enjoy painting and not mind being in a fully contained suit while working in small bathroom areas.

HB: Training is acquired from an existing company located far away from your intended area. A three day seminar is offered and can be found on the internet. Most likely, the training course is not located in your state. Be prepared to pay for the course, travel, meals and motel costs. Refinishing tubs requires repeated practice to avoid runs and over spraying. The chemicals used to refinish tubs are highly toxic, yet very effective. A fresh air respirator and a full jumpsuit are required at all times. Customers pets and anyone with a health condition may not be anywhere around during refinishing and for a full day afterwards.

The industry has a poor reputation because sometimes the coating peels up soon after the job is completed. This is 100% caused by poor workmanship! To the untrained eye, the difference between quality work and a poor job is hardly noticeable until months later. One reason is that some customers will shop only for price regardless of who does the work. Advertise in a local Apartment owner's type of magazine. Some realtors create these newsletter type magazines to keep their name in front of the owners. Do a search and you should find the appropriate advertising magazine. Also, a small display advertisement in the business services directory.

P: The way to be successful is to refuse to compete with lowball pricing. Do ethical, honest work every time. In a very short time, you will have enough work from referrals alone. The only advertising you will need is your name and phone number in the business directory without an expensive display advertisement.

OPE: About $1500. For brand new equipment (if used cannot be located), paints and supplies plus training.

Start Your Business with Very Little Money

MI: Find the most sociable people you know. The person that's always in the middle of every social event, super talkative and couldn't be quiet to save their life, you already have someone in mind! Offer such a discount that they just couldn't refuse. If they LOVE your work, hand them a stack of business cards. That's it, that's all you need, *if you do a great Job!*

Buy and Sell Vehicles
W: Buy vehicles for much less than wholesale prices and resell closer to the actual value.

SN: Negotiating skills, salesmanship, penny pinching (they add up), thinking and talking at the same time and the desire to do thorough research over every detail.

HB: Safety First! Be aware of the people you're dealing with. Ask to see their drivers' license "for the paper work". Anytime a buyer or seller mentions that; they're "in a hurry", a red flag goes up in my head. Never have the vehicle title or cash in your pocket on a first meeting. It's always a good idea to bring someone along. When returning calls to unknown individuals; question those phone numbers that seem to always go straight to voice mail and they call you back. Ask for another phone number. Be bold and clear with pointed questions. You should get reassurance and no sign of evasion or gray area responses. Go with your instincts. If it doesn't feel right, delay or cancel the meeting until you're comfortable.

Avoid Traps, on first inspection, remember to write down the license plate number and check the expiration date. Write down the Vehicle Identification Number (VIN) and call or visit the local Motor Vehicles Department to check for unpaid tickets, liens and "salvage Title". A vehicle history report may be worth the investment as you can show your future prospective buyer the same report.

Consider exchanging title for funds from buyers inside their bank. Your bank may accept a phony Money Order or Forged check at the time; later, when the fraud is revealed, they will hold YOU accountable with the guilty person long gone and untraceable with no recourse. Lastly, Check the VIN plate for tampering and, if possible, the engine serial number. Again, if something is too good to be true, it usually is.

Be objective, in the heat of the moment, we sometimes overlook the obvious flaws during the examination and negotiations. There are purposeful distractions at opportune times-when a seller wants to sell. Take another hard look.

Be an expert, knowing everything about certain makes and models that you intend to buy and sell, will give you an advantage over others. You will already know where to find potential problems and; what the true resell value is from the condition and mileage of the vehicle.

Prepare for resale: Detail (cleaning and polishing) the vehicle thoroughly, it's an absolute must. If needed: get new floor mats, faux rims and nice smelling sprays. They can be purchased at any auto parts store. Take plenty of photos at different angles (inside and out) and choose the best ones. Use exciting and upbeat descriptions with lots of details when writing your ad.

Where to Sell: Traderonline.com and anywhere you can post or publish your pictures with the rich descriptions. Drive the vehicle around town with a fresh "for sale" sign. Park your vehicle on busy streets. Talk to a gas station owner and offer to pay him if he allows you to put it in a highly visible spot for a few weeks. The high traffic of a gas station should sell the vehicle much quicker and at a better price.

P: Keep in mind that most people have a limited amount of cash to purchase a vehicle. Over a certain amount, they have to get financed. Financing takes time and is usually only available to people with good credit. The more affordable you can sell the vehicle for, the wider the net is cast for a potential buyer.

OPE: The cost of your first vehicle (after thorough research to ensure you're paying a below wholesale price), cosmetic and minor mechanical repairs and advertising costs.

MI: Best Places to Buy Vehicles:

1. Any internet or print advertisement without a photo and/ or little description. The current owner isn't putting much effort into selling the vehicle and would possibly accept a lower offer.
2. Old "for sale" signs on vehicles in less traveled areas.
3. Print publications at the moment they are distributed. Call each news paper, recycler, Penny saver and Auto trader for distribution days, times and locations to get your copy "hot off the press".
4. Some internet websites have a feature that will automatically notify you by email of every new posting for the make and model you are seeking in your desired area.

Carpet Cleaning

W: Clean carpets, drapes, blinds and furniture at businesses, homes and apartments.

SN: Patience, desire to do a thorough job and an "easy to get along with" personality.

HB: Acquire used professional carpet cleaning equipment through the equipment trader magazines, an internet search or calling out of town companies for excess equipment. Get training with a company, or; get the operation manual from the equipment manufacturer and practice with trial and error on your friends and family carpets. Commercial carpet cleaning equipment is available to rent by the day, but cuts deep into your profit. Doing decent work at reasonable rates will net you the same customers two, three, maybe four times a year, plus referrals from each customer.

P: To get a true picture of what the competition is charging, talk to several people who have a work order/ receipt/ estimate from competitors. Many will advertise one price, but will be far different than the actual cost the customer eventually pays. Cleaning jobs at businesses are usually charged per square foot of carpet. Apartments will pay a flat rate. Call your competition to see what they quote over the phone. Try to corner an <u>employee</u> at a convenience store and casually talk to him about the facts.

Start Your Business with Very Little Money

OPE: Start up costs depends on how good of a deal you get on your used commercial equipment is and cleaning chemicals.

MI: Decide who will be your primary customer, business or residential. Businesses will be steadier, but the work will be mostly after hours and they usually pay less and you have to wait for a check up to 45 days later and liability insurance must be paid for by you. Residential customers pay more, right away but work can be very slow or extremely busy.

Child Care Provider
W: Care   for   children   in   your   home.
SN: Nurturing and caring desire for children. Have a safe, clean environment place to provide the service.

HB: Check your city, county or state for requirements to provide this service. They may require everyone in the house to have a background check and your home may need to be inspected by the health department. Your home will need to be made kid safe. With so many working mothers today, this is a growing business. There is a lot of profit in caring for children, as you may know, child care is expensive. There is hardly a need to advertise, maybe place a small display ad in the business services directory. Most of your business will be word of mouth. Once you have enough kids, create a waiting list.

P: depending on your area, $100-150 a week for pre-school kids and half that for school aged children who come, (or you pick up) after school. Call your competitors to compare prices.

OPE: The cost to make your home safe for kids and the time and effort to meet government requirements.

MI: A handful of flyers to homes in your neighborhood. In most areas, there is demand for decent and clean child care providers.

Chimney Sweeper
W: Clean chimneys for homes and businesses.

Start Your Business with Very Little Money

SN: Not afraid of heights on steep roofs, have a spouse that loves you even though you come home covered in black soot (and a pocketful of money) everyday.

HB: There is a six day training course available for roughly $600 plus motel, food and travel expenses. The course is in Indiana and can be found with an internet search. The course gives you an important "certified" status. Place small, inexpensive advertising in the business services directory and any neighborhood oriented publication. Once you have established your business, the same customers will call you year after year.

P: Average charge varies from $100 to $200+. A typical chimney takes about an hour. There is an extra charge for spark arresting vent caps and repairs the customer may need.

OPE: Training $600 plus, depending on how far you travel to Indiana and how frugal you manage your money during that week. Equipment and start up advertising should cost $1500 to $2500.

MI: Prepare a "media kit" for local newspaper, radio and television stations. The media kit should include all the information about chimney fires. They may use it and quote your company **when** the next one happens in your area. Include your contact information with an offer to be interviewed by a reporter. You can also offer to give a cleaning demonstration on one of your customers' homes. Rehearse over and over how you plan to represent your company and what kind of information you will be giving. The idea is; as a member of the community, share your knowledge about the subject, not to take advantage of someone else's loss, but trying to prevent the *next* one from happening.

Clothing Designer

W: Design any type of clothing, accessories, sandals and/ or hat that is unique and can not be bought anywhere else.

SN: Have an artistic flair; be up on styles and what the teenagers and young adults are wearing. Know how to operate a sewing machine, be willing to learn or pay someone to sew for you.

HB: There are really cool sewing and embroidery machines on the

Start Your Business with Very Little Money

market now. You can conceive anything on a computer and have it made. There are plenty of seamstresses that can be found at your local sewing supply and fabric store to make your prototypes.

Your job is to create the clothing that will look good and sell. If you notice the trends, there is very little difference between a bland shirt or top and an awesome one. Maybe it's shaped or cut just a little different, maybe too many people have that type of shirt or top and it doesn't appeal to most people anymore. Also, trends resurface every ten to twenty years. Find the next returning trend and put a modern twist to the clothing and you have the hottest items on the market. Some designers get a popular trend going by using the newest type of fabric or by using an existing fabric in a way that no one has thought of yet.

Any tee shirt can be screen printed from your design and artwork from a tee shirt printing business. One would cost over $100, but make 100 and the price can drop to less than $5 each.

Make clothing for your friends as well as yourself and get feedback to what people are saying about the look. You will know if you have a winning trend if other people are asking you to make one for them too. A commercial sewing company can make clothing quickly and inexpensively. Find a few and get quotes from manufacturers on different quantities and sizes. You will know what each unit will cost and figure your profit from your best selling price. When you can afford to pay for the smallest run from a manufacturer, consider starting your own web page that people can order from and begin to offer your items to clothing stores in your area.

After some success, find the next textile show in your area and rent a booth for a weekend. The show manager will help you figure out what you need to bring and have at the booth. Most likely; business cards, order contracts, a table, banner and several samples ready to give to people who actually sign a contract with you right then, and need to bring back a sample for their headquarters. You may have orders beyond your wildest imagination. You could also offer to sell the design(s) outright to anyone for a quick profit.

P: Original clothing cost much more than store bought clothing. People who purchase your styles will realize that they have a one of a kind and be willing to pay much more.

OPE: $200-500 designing and making your clothes. Afterwards, you should be able to sell the clothing for more money than it costs to make.

MI: Don't try too hard! Outlandish clothing hardly ever becomes fashionable. Pay attention to what looks right and weather or not YOU like it. Gimmicky clothing is fine to draw attention to your line of products, just don't expect it to sell or sell well.

Club Promoter

W: There are clubs and bars that have hardly any customers on some *or* most nights. A promoter is a person who makes an agreement with the owner to be paid a percentage above what that place usually earns for a typical night. The promoter spends his/ her own money on entertainment, decorations, advertising, disc jockeys and events to bring in the customers. Sometimes, a door charge is split between the promoter and owner.

SN: Sociable to the extreme. Be able and willing to talk to anyone at anytime about anything. Share enthusiasm by helping others feel comfortable and that *they* are with the "in crowd" at any event you create.

HB: Learn about what other club promoters are doing in your area and what is successful. You will probably find that the personality of the promoter is what makes him or her so successful, regardless of the event. To gather your own "following", make as many friends as you can every night you go out, just be genuine, every time. The more you introduce people to each other, the better. They go to clubs and bars to see and be seen AND to socialize and you are an instant friend to almost anyone you reach out to. They will follow you to any event; because, at least, you'll be there. Word of mouth, like a personal invitation, is much better than placing a flyer on every car in the parking lots of every neighboring clubs.

Be absolutely sure about who you do business with; in the entertainment and the club owner/ manager. Your reputation is at stake at every event, even from situations that you have little or no control of, in the beginning. Some people like the drama of other peoples' personality conflicts, as long as none of those personalities are violent!

Depending on what type of personality you have; anything from dart and pool tournaments to down and dirty dance party atmospheres can be created and hyped if you're totally into that scene.

OPE: Advertising buzz can get pricy from ads in "cool" local publications and radio stations. The more "friends" you make by laying the ground work first, the less money will be needed for advertising.

MI: Create your own signature event. An example would be: "The Redneck Bikini Cousins"- "hosts: fog in night" at the "..... Club" There are plenty of exhibitionist attractive females who would gladly *volunteer* to be a "Redneck Bikini Cousin". The Cousins get in for free and gain some local popularity! Don't forget to include a *really* hideous Cousin who has a great sense of humor. Create a routine with them and ask them to perform it once, late in the evening at each event. People will hang around and wait to see it, even if it's just a few minutes long. Some people *want* a reason to stay awhile longer even though you're already entertaining them. A couple of fogging machines would set you back a hundred dollars that you can use over and over. Call radio stations about those wacky redneck bikini cousins being at the "....Club" tonight! You make the party, wherever you are, is where it's at.

Copier Repair Service

W: Almost every single business has a copier machine. They are full of electronics and mechanical parts that need servicing and repair.

SN: Work for a copier repair company <u>that services all makes and models</u>.

HB: You must learn, at least, the basics of each model. There are classes that some manufacturers provide on how to repair and service their products. They are not free and you will probably have to travel to their location. You can get manuals from most manufacturers. They are not free. Call manufacturers to inquire about their class schedule for future classes and cost per class. Even though this business takes a lot of time for training, the pay is excellent and work is very steady.

Start Your Business with Very Little Money

OPE: The tools and electronic testing equipment $200-400.

MI: Sign up every new customer with a service contract to provide monthly maintenance and emergency repairs. The contract is usually based on the typical amount of copies they use per month.

Disabled & Senior Home Modification Specialist

W: When a person is injured or disabled from an illness or accident, they are eventually released from the hospital and sent home. There are many needs and challenges for them to adjust temporarily or permanently to their new health condition. Some need ramps over steps, grab bars in bathrooms, special bathroom sinks to maneuver their wheel chairs underneath, special toilets for necessity, hospital beds set up, hanging bars to grab onto, non slip strips placed on slippery tile floors and on and on. It all depends on their mobility and needs. America's population is aging. The baby boomers are beginning to retire. There will be a growing need for this type of service.

SN: Empathy for their predicament, thorough research on code requirements for disabled access, equipment available and "contractor grade" handyman skills.

HB: There is a manual available from the "International Association of Plumbing and Mechanical Officials" regarding accessibility requirements. The guidelines help you to help the customer decide what modifications they need and want. Be aware that some customers will not have the funds readily available to pay for your services. Some will be waiting for insurance checks, lawsuit settlements, donations from their church, and refinancing of homes due to their loss of income. Offer as many payment plans and financing options as you can to provide your services. Your willingness to be flexible will gain extra work when others walk away. Advertise in the local business directory and make contacts in the medical field for referrals. There probably isn't even a section in the business directory phone book yet. Be the first and ask the representative to create the heading. They can and usually will. Get free equipment catalogs and installation manuals from accessibility manufacturers. Study the equipment available and basic prices to be ready to offer to your customer. If you begin to purchase in large

66

quantities, the manufacturer may allow you to become a local distributor. By becoming a distributor, you will save as much as 50% off list prices.

P: Charge at least 10 to 20% more for labor and materials than a basic handyman; due to being specialized in modifications. You will *still* be cheaper than the competition because you will be saving time from experience and not be over estimating materials and equipment prices.

OPE: Purchasing manuals and advertising, besides having handyman experience.

MI: Send every accident attorney a letter and business card describing your services and payment terms. Contact your local social services department and senior center to establish a relationship. Learn how to become a qualified contractor for your local government agency.

Document Destruction Services
W: Companies, by law, must keep detailed records for a number of years. The information on those documents is confidential and poses legal problems if they are not destroyed properly.

HB: Document destruction companies are insured to destroy the files and papers properly. All employees will need background checks and be bonded. A city license should be mandatory. You will need to prove to the insurance company that you will be conducting business properly. A written manual on your company procedures and the equipment you will be using will need to be submitted. Employee uniforms, professional vehicle signs and your advertising materials must exude professionalism to gain customer confidence.

Advertise in the business to business directory as well as the standard business directory phone book. There are great advertising places in local magazines specifically aimed at the elite high class business managers and owners. Walk into several corporate headquarters waiting rooms in your area and you'll begin to notice them. The only way to learn this business is to become hired by an out of the area employer. Be sure you do not sign a "non-compete" agreement.

Start Your Business with Very Little Money

Some companies will have hundreds of thousands of dollars worth of vehicles and equipment for efficiency. By learning their process, you can create a scaled down version to get started. Remember that you will be getting paid twice for your services. The business will pay you to destroy the documents and the recyclers will pay you for the shredded materials. To get the best prices from the recycler, you will need to provide the businesses with separate disposal bins for different types of paper. Document shredding machines can be located in the business to business phone book, internet search and auctions.

P: Price will need to be at or lower than the competition with more services included.

OPE: Research finding good used equipment. As many businesses are failing, their office equipment is literally selling for pennies to their original purchase price. Shop around continuously until you find out where they are selling professional shredding and office equipment in your area.

MI: Advertise in the local business directory phone book an unbelievably low, low price of $10 for up to 100 lbs. of home pick up document destruction*. When they call for the details (*) You will pick up their documents on your schedule and day to maximize your pick up route (their schedule is extra charge), no staples, paper clips or any type of metal (extra charge) and any more than 100 lbs, is at regular pricing. Many company managers will see your offer and will consider your company for their (thousands of pounds worth of) business.

Drain Cleaning Service
W: Clearing stopped up drains and sewer pipes in homes and businesses.

SN: Experience is a must as the drain cleaning machines can be dangerous and tricky to operate. Must not be squeamish about this type of work (takes getting use to) and getting dirty from oiled machines and, well...sewage. Being completely sanitary at all times is nearly impossible due to some confined spaces and work areas.

HB: This type of work is easily learned from an out of the area plumbing/ drain cleaning company that specializes (advertises) drain cleaning. After a few months of full time employment, you will most likely have the experience to (at least) avoid hurting yourself and damaging the customers' property.

Used equipment is hard to find but is available occasionally. There are three types of drain cleaning machines. A drill snake has a cable that is about a quarter of an inch thick. They cost about $250 -$300 new. A drill snake is used to clear tub drains, bathroom sinks and sometimes kitchen sinks. A standard drain cleaning machine has a cable (snake) about 3/8 – 5/8 thick. It costs $350- $700, depending on the features and the manufacturer. Standard drain cleaning equipment is used for pipes from 1 ½" to 3". Mainline sewer machines costs around $900-$1400 and is used strictly for the main sewer line, when everything in the house is backed up.

Mainline machines can be very dangerous to the unskilled. A toilet auger cost around $50 for a professional quality unit and operates manually. Some equipment rental places have drain cleaning available for rent. In desperate times, an agreement may be made with the rental company for a substantial discounted rate if you frequently rent equipment. Both of you win.

There are many tricks to the trade. All the difficulty learning makes you more of a specialist and prods the homeowner to call you instead of doing it himself. When the problem is a broken or collapsed pipe, refer the job to a trusted plumber, who will in turn, include your service call charge in his repair bill and reimburse you afterwards. After you have built up a customer base, you should earn a substantial living as drain cleaning is recession proof. Advertise in the penny saver and other local neighborhood mailers.

P: Starting out, your pricing must be overly competitive while offering better, cleaner, friendlier and faster services to build up your customer base. Once you are busy 3 out of 5 days a week, you can begin to slowly raise your prices for new customers.

OPE: Start with a drill snake, a standard snake and a toilet auger. Turn down mainline stoppages or rent the machine when needed until you can afford to purchase one. Buy used if you're lucky enough to locate a good machine at a good price. The minimum equipment required is about $1500 to start.

Start Your Business with Very Little Money

MI: Liberally pass out refrigerator magnets to kids, friends, their friend's kids, their kids' friends etc. They will cost about $.15 each. One call for every hundred passed out, pays for them and makes this a very cheap and effective advertising method. Purchase custom designed and printed magnets online for best pricing. They will end up in unexpected places; they're cheap and fun for everyone.

Drinking Water Filter Replacement Service

W: Many homes and businesses have drinking water filters and osmosis systems. Many don't know how, or are incapable (due to their age and strength) of replacing cartridges, filters, clean osmosis filters and give the system a basic check up. Almost no one knows how to repair the system if it doesn't function properly. A few companies service just their own brand. There is hardly any competition for this type of service.

SN: Be mechanically inclined and willing to learn how to service and repair different systems.

HB: There are numerous manufacturers of filter and osmosis systems. Many filters are interchangeable. The same filter will have a different part number for each osmosis/ water filter system manufacturer but was originally purchased from the same <u>filter</u> manufacturer. Purchase manuals and parts lists from every osmosis/ water filter system manufacturer you can find. Locate the FILTER MANUFACTURERS and get their price list. Compare the filters in the systems for duplicates with different part numbers and purchase those filters directly from the filter manufacturer for a fraction of what the system manufacturer charges. Resale the items at the system manufacturers price and profit the difference from buying in bulk also, along with the service charge for labor.

To learn, offer to service and/ or repair anyone's system for free if they pay for the filters and parts, provided they understand that you are learning along the way. Repair parts may take a week to get. After tinkering with several different types and studying the different manuals, you will understand the basic workings and the most common types of parts and filters that you will need. Some equipment manufacturers offer a training seminar for their complete line of systems Water testing equipment should be purchased. A water quality test is important to check the water system or to help sell potential new installations.

Offer to drive to customers homes to inspect their systems and get the manufacturers name and model number as you may need to order certain specialized filters. Some systems have numerous filters in the same system. Most likely, that system will have at least one or more common type of filter that can be replaced on your first visit. Keep detailed records of each customers system and the filter installation date. Inform the customer of the manufacturers' recommendations on the time between filter changes and ask them if they would like to maintain that schedule. If so, send a postcard to the customer a couple of weeks prior to that date to schedule an appointment with your company.

This is a highly specialized type of service. Be prepared to travel as far as you are capable of driving round trip and servicing a few units in a single day. A small advertisement in the business services directory phone book in several areas you are willing to drive is recommended. Remember that each area phone book will most likely be distributed at different times of the year.

This business will take patience in learning the different systems; establishing the proper quantities and types of inventory you should carry and allowing yourself time to build up enough customers to be profitable. Once established, the same customers can be serviced repeatedly. Only a few new customers will be needed each year to replace the ones that move away or cancel their service.

Attempt to become an authorized repair company for system manufacturers, even if they pay you very little for a service call. You will get your foot in the door and probably get called to replace their filters later. Each system should take a half hour or less to clean and replace filters.

P: This is a highly specialized business and there probably isn't any comparison in competition. Due to the travel times and specialization, I recommend charging an amount that is just high enough to make you uncomfortable saying it out loud (at first).

Start Your Business with Very Little Money

OPE: There will be some trial and error in gathering the proper filters and repair parts. Some systems are more popular than others in different parts of the country, if you buy large quantities of the less popular parts and filters, they may last you your whole career in the filter business. Filters can be expensive so tread lightly at first, even if it costs you a few customers. Be prepared to spend $1000 or more on filters and basic repair parts. The good news is that no truck is needed. All repair parts, filters and tools should fit easily in any car trunk. An economy car will save fuel costs in traveling large distances.

MI: Follow the money. Upper income neighborhoods and professional buildings are your main customers. There may be many middle class customers, but many will change their own filters, after watching you make it look so effortless and quick. In every area, there are local magazines focused on the "well to do" and their needs. Besides the business services directory phone book, consider placing small advertisements in those types of local magazines. Remember to order advertising stickers to place on every filter system, "FOR SERVICE, OR FILTER REPLACEMENT BY ---/----/ --- date, CALL (555)555-5555.

Dry Cleaning Business (store front and mobile)
W: Many dry cleaning businesses are nothing but a store front with a counter, cash register and a wall with racks for the clothing in the back. Some dry cleaning companies just have a pick up and delivery van, all the business is done with credit cards and orders placed over the phone or with order slips filled out at the customers' door.

There are commercial dry cleaning plants located throughout the country and one may be near you. The commercial plants dry clean and launder clothing for small "store front" operations that pick up and deliver their customers clothing to the plant. Even if there is no big commercial plant near you, find a dry cleaning store in a nearby town and negotiate prices to process your customers items at bulk rates. They already have the equipment and employees in place.

SN: Be familiar with dry cleaning operations. Work at a drycleaners, preferably away from the area you plan to conduct business.

Start Your Business with Very Little Money

HB: Your biggest expense (and risk) is leasing store space at a local shopping center. A nice, used clean van with a new paint job and professional sign can be obtained for very little money.

P: Be competitive.(see MI) .

OPE: A store front lease in a shopping center. Or, a cargo van with graphics on the side. PLUS, a few thousand dollars is needed for advertising, printing and racks to hang the clothes on.

MI: Repeatedly offer a neighborhood discount that is at your break even point to get the locals to use your new dry cleaning company. When you have enough customers, phase out the coupons and discounts.

Duct Cleaning Service

W: Duct cleaning involves furnace cleaning and filter replacement, dryer vent clearing and cleaning, as well as removing dust and debris from air conditioning and heating ducts. People with allergies, pets, children, health issues or are moving into an older house get their ducts cleaned to improve the quality of the inside air and remove odors.

A "weed whacker" type of wand, attached to an air hose is fed into the ducts from each vent towards the furnace. A HEPA vacuum is attached to the furnace and sealed. The weed whacker knocks all the dust and debris free while the heap vacuum sucks it away. Afterwards, the furnace is completely cleaned and a new filter is installed. Vent covers usually have multiple layers of old paint and look beaten up. New vents are offered to the customer for an additional charge.

SN: Familiarity with duct work, mechanically inclined, doesn't mind getting a little dirty, salesmanship and patience.

HB: Equipment and training can be obtained from the manufacturer for about $20,000. Used equipment could be found for ten to twenty percent of that price. Duct cleaning is very specialized and requires patience and constant advertising. Some people get frustrated through the ups and downs and just want to get out, so they sell off the equipment for almost nothing. Training can be learned through trial and error and reading the manufacturers instructions.

Start Your Business with Very Little Money

I recommend spending an equal amount of money on new vent covers in multiple sizes to carry with you on each job. This is a popular up-sell but is useless if you don't have enough or the right sizes to install immediately. There are many different vent cover sizes. Only the correct size will fit each vent. One home could have 12 to 20 of one specific size. Always check the sizes first. Once you know you have the stock to offer to replace them all (or most), hold a new one in one hand and the worst looking one in the other, then ask if they would like to replace them all. One look at the comparison of the two will almost guarantee an instant sale.

Plenty of drop cloths are needed to cover over every area you are in, basically the whole house. Great care must be taken to cut the paint cleanly to separate each vent from the wall. While in the house, you should be very ginger and proceed carefully to not even bump any wall or table with your ladders. The type of customer that uses duct cleaning services is orderly, clean and sensitive to any little mark, stain or paint chip on their home and possessions.

Advertising should be directed to the upper class neighborhoods, businesses and private schools (for health reasons). A small display advertisement, that is cheap enough to consistently run, could be placed in local upscale magazines. A small ad should be placed in the business services directory phone books as far as you could drive in one day while working only two to three hours for one job.

Be sure to exude professionalism at all times; in person and in advertising. This is so specialized that you may be the only one offering this service in your area. An annual maintenance contract should be offered to every customer. They sign and agree to have their vents cleaned every year; you send a post card and call to schedule a few weeks before to set the appointment.

P: I, personally, would charge <u>at least</u> $395 for an average home, plus charge $100 over my cost for new vent covers. Keep in mind that your average advertising cost *could* be up to half of your profit for each job until you're established. One home should take about two hours to service, plus travel time.

Start Your Business with Very Little Money

OPE: Start up costs depend heavily on what the new equipment is purchased for. If you are able to find and purchase the equipment for a comfortable price and still leave yourself money for business set-up and advertising, and; you can give yourself time to build customers, then go for it!

MI: Send, or better yet, walk into every plumbing company and air conditioning Company with six advertising magnets and six business cards with a personalized letter describing your business and price list. Offer the company your services as *their* subcontractor with your suggested rates (100%) and their (they pay you 75% and they profit 25%) discounted rates. They offer the service to their customers, you do the work and up-sell the vent covers (you sell for full price and get 75% of the extra charges). They collect, (or you collect for them with the check made out to the A/C or plumbing company) and you get reimbursed. If you spend half of your profits on advertising to get your own customers; you will earn you much more whenever you are providing your services as their subcontractor.

Relationships and trust will need to be built. They will be cautious when trusting you with their customers. Expect several attempts and several trips to their company before they give you one shot. Make sure the first time goes extremely smooth for everyone involved. You could offer to wear their company uniform or shirt while at the customers home or business.

Fence and Gate Installer
W: Install chain link, wood and PVC plastic fences and gates.

SN: Wood working skills, measuring, good at fractions and math, are able to manhandle large sections of fencing. Be handy with the power tools.

HB: You can find installation methods on the internet or in "how to" books for just about any type of fencing. To start, advertise in the penny saver type of magazine. The customers will be require a low price, so they should be more patient on how long the job takes you. They also should be understanding and allow you time to correct the mistakes you will definitely make the first time you install any type of fence.

P: When estimating your first jobs, figure $30 an hour plus materials. After you are fast and efficient, up to $100 an hour plus materials. Give them a flat price and do not separate materials from the labor. If they persist in asking you to separate the prices, inform them that you have a built in buffer for materials and labor overruns, but not both at the same time. If they would like separate prices, you need to add a buffer separately on each price, in case they would like to locate and purchase the materials themselves.

OPE: You should have most of the tools needed. A come-a –long is required for installing chain liked fencing. Purchase a used one at a flea market.

MI: Build display samples for home shows and fairs. Purchase a booth for the weekend and have prospective customers fill out estimate requests. There are many home improvement companies who get most of their work from home shows. Visit the next show in your area and talk to the shows' manager for rate information and requirements.

Finders Fee

W: Investors and buyers purchase expensive items like homes, vehicles and jewelry. They hold the item to resell later for much more than they paid for the item. Investors will gladly pay you a finder's fee of about one percent for bringing them great deals.

SN: Present yourself as professional; having manners, class and honesty in tempting situations. Like sales, be continuously looking for opportunities and talking to many people.

HB: Find the investors. In the newspaper, sometimes there are ads posted "Will buy your home in 24 hours!" This is a real estate investor. Similar ads for different items can be found when you start looking. Look in the "Wanted to Buy" section of vehicle sales magazines. Investors usually specialize in one type of item. You should consider specializing in one thing too. Learning the value and the reasons *why* something is worth more or less takes time. When introducing yourself to an investor over the phone, ask them if they would pay you a finder's fee for a good, legitimate deal; and, what kinds of property (or items) they like to purchase. Once the investor knows he can trust you, most of them will agree to do business with you and will pay you the fee once the deal is completed.

P: Typically one percent but everything is negotiable.

OPE: Time and gas. There is no start up fees.

MI: If you hear about somebody who received an inheritance, sometimes they have no interest in the property or items inherited and would much rather have the cash. Many times, you can facilitate a sale by helping them find the best buyer to meet their needs. You screen the buyers, but only consider those that will pay (and sign an agreement) your fee for your efforts. Check your state and local laws for any restrictions.

Garage Door Repair and Replacement

W: Repair garage doors, electric openers and replace older models.

SN: Mechanically inclined. Have a truck with a lumber rack to bring new doors and haul away old ones.

HB: Training is best received from working for an out of the area garage door company. You could learn from trial and error, but expect your education to take twice as long and be more frustrating for you and your customers. Many garage doors are manufactured in China. If you don't mind selling Chinese made products, you should be able to purchase a whole container full of garage doors for almost half of what you will pay your wholesaler (see importing). Chinese companies can be found on alibaba.com. Until then, find a relatively close wholesaler in your area when working for another company or perform a persistent internet search and make some calls. Garage door openers and some repair parts can be found at the local home improvement store, just to get you started. You should locate every door (and parts) supplier anyway, but some will have a minimum order policy. Advertise in the business services directory phone book and local home magazines in small, affordable display ads.

P: Some garage door companies are advertising $395 for a plain garage door installed, not including the motorized opener. Be competitive to your local market. Old garage doors are hauled away for an extra charge.

OPE: The minimum order quantity from the wholesaler. Parts and openers can be purchased from the home improvement store until you can afford to buy in bulk.

MI: Get your advertising sticker on every opener motor and door you can. Mail a personalized letter with a special discount and be sure to include magnets and stickers. Consider working with property managers and landlords at a discounted rate until regular residential customers start calling. Always put your service sticker on every garage door, even at free estimates.

Glass Man/ Shower Door Repairs and Installation

W: Replacing broken windows at homes and businesses. Also replacing and installing new shower doors and mirrors.

SN: You **MUST have experience.** Glass can cut you to the bone in an instant! Many people have died or been seriously injured from carrying and installing glass. Get employed with a distant company and learn everything first.

HB: Choose what part of the glass industry you would like to specialize in.
Some glass men specialize in shower doors and mirrors; others enjoy working at commercial buildings. You specialize in one area but service the rest. Advertise in the business services directory under the heading you like to specialize in.

P: Be competitive until you build up word of mouth and establish some commercial accounts.

OPE: Working at homes will require less operating capital since you will be paid immediately after each job. Business accounts typically pay 30-45 days later. Tools are a minor expense $200-350.

MI: Contact bathroom remodeling companies to work as their subcontractor. Sometimes shower doors are complex and must be measured and installed precisely. If there is a mistake, the glass panels are trashed and the correctly sized panel is reordered (up to a few weeks for manufacturing and shipping). The remodeling contractors are interested in having the glass installed right the first time, without delays.

Hauling Service

W: People need old appliances, furniture, yard debris, ex-spouses things, dirt etc hauled away. Not everybody has or wants a friend with a pick up to get rid of stuff for them. Some people are too frail, don't have the time or there's too much of it to do. There is a need.

SN: Physically fit and want to stay that way and have a pick up truck. You must not mind getting dirty.

HB: You can even begin with a mini truck if necessary. Buy or find two 4x8 sheets of low quality plywood and if you have the inserts on your truck bed for 2x4's (three on each side), buy a few 2"x4"x8's. Cut out a section on each of the 4x8 sheets for the wheel wells. You will have four feet high sides from the bottom of your truck bed to the top of the plywood. Try out one and stick a 2x4 into one of the insert holes. Mark the 2x4 where the plywood ends with a pencil and cut the 2x4. Use some wood screws to screw the 2x4's to the 4x8 sheets. Do the same for the rest of the holes. Now you have a 4' high, Buy or find some sturdy rope, tarp, shovel, rake, broom and dust pan. You are ready to work. Later, a wheel barrow and a dolly can be obtained.

Make an effort to leave the area raked or swept clean. Know *every* single place you can dispose trash, recycle (read recycling service) and dump clean dirt, asphalt, concrete, paints and chemicals legally in the areas where you plan to work. Get the disposal fees memorized to make estimating easier.

Advertise with the Penny Saver and a small business directory phone book listing. Create a flyer and clip business cards to each one. Personally pass out the flyers, to every property management company (commercial and residential), self storage facility, apartment complex and any company you can think of that could use your service. No single advertising publication will be adequate to support you (unless you're lucky).

P: There are three parts to every estimate you give. A) What is the overall weight for the dump fees? Your guesstimate times 1.5 to C.Y.A. B) How many trips to the disposal facility? Based on the weight and amount that my truck can hold and the cost of fuel. C) How many man hours X hourly pay of $25, 30 or 35 an hour will this take?

Quoting prices takes courage to muster up at first, but be firm. Remember that you need to pay for your phone, advertising, and maintenance for your truck and income taxes on all of your profit. It is painful to work hard all month and find out you earned minimum wages after paying your expenses. Your businesses will survive and thrive if you charge fair prices for both <u>you and the customer</u>.

OPE: Less than $100 plus advertising, printing and gas to pass out flyers.

MI: People dispose of many valuable items during move outs, divorces, consolidation of storage units, etc. They pay you to haul it away. Separate anything you think you could sell and take the gathered items once a month to a local flea market/ swap meet. The weekend profits can add up to an extra $1000 or more a month!

Importing Products
W: Find products from overseas manufacturers that you sell here to local buyers.

SN: Research capabilities, patience with ESL people, sheer determination in searching for the exact product. Good credit for short term financing.

HB: Go to alibaba.com (or similar web sites) and do searches for the product you are looking to import. There is plenty of neat stuff to look at that isn't available here. In dealing with the manufacturers' salesman, many will not return your email on your first attempt. Sometimes they aren't interested in dealing with someone new asking about limited quantities, price, and new ventures...whatever. Your determination and persistence will pay off, eventually. Sometimes they respond immediately and are helpful from the beginning.

Start Your Business with Very Little Money

After establishing the exact product, price and minimum quantity required to order; Ask the manufacturers representative to send you a couple of samples of each item you are interested in, at your expense. YOU MUST DO THIS. <u>You must get the exact item, without any future changes to anything, in your hands to inspect.</u> If there are to be any changes, wait for the final product to be in your hands prior to showing it to any buyer. I know of two people who were burned badly in this type of transaction. To ship samples, the manufacturer will require you to wire about $100 US for a couple of items worth less than $2-4. They email you their banking information. You go to your bank, fill out a form and hand the teller your money. It's worth it! They typically send it DHL or FedEx and you receive the samples in a few days.

Some chain stores have an open door policy that allows salesmen (you) to come in once a week on a certain day to offer the product(s) for sale. Take your samples there. Know the exact minimum order (you will be required to purchase, at least, a small container, 20'x8'x8', of product.) that is the number you need to sell, or multiples of that number. Not a little more or a little less, unless you wish to pay for, and sell the rest on your own.

Make absolutely certain what, if any tariffs will be imposed by the government (customs, check their website and/or call). Make absolutely certain you have, in writing, from a licensed import agent (check major delivery companies, as some handle the whole transportation from the manufacturers dock to your buyers dock) the exact amount that trucking will cost from the dock to their distribution warehouse, and the exact amount for shipping the container to the U.S. You must have hard numbers on unit costs, tariff and transportation costs in order to know what your lowest price is when offering to sell to stores. Many stores will allow you enough time between signing the contract and the scheduled delivery; to get the deal funded by a bank and have the products made and shipped from China.

After signing a contract with a store to purchase your items, take the paperwork to your bank. Speak to a business banker to arrange a short term loan to pay for the manufacturing and shipping. It would be wise to get the exact costs of what your bank will charge to make this short term loan. In fact, get pre-approved with hard numbers prior to making a deal if you are concerned. There are other companies that make these kinds of loans too.

P: Do the math, over and over. Check and recheck everything. Get everything in writing from everyone involved.

OPE: If you plan on paying for everything without a short term loan, your start up costs could be anywhere from $10-50,000. Otherwise, your start up costs is less than $200 plus gas and time to locate buyers.

MI: If you're having trouble locating a single buyer for your whole container, locate several or more individual customers who will order in smaller quantities. Be sure to sell at least 10% more than you actually order, due to some buyers canceling during the wait. In order to get funding from a bank, get each buyer to sign an agreement to purchase the quantity they desire. While sitting in the waiting room of any chain store, be as sociable as possible with other salesmen. They will give you helpful pricing tips, possibly give you leads to other kinds of stores that would be interested in your product, or actually sell it for you for a percentage. Have several cards ready to hand out. You may be more successful in the waiting room, even if that particular store turns you down.

Janitorial Services
W: Smaller businesses and properties use outside janitorial services to clean their office buildings, association "common use" pool bathrooms and meeting areas, apartment building common areas and preparing vacancies for rental.
SN: Have attention to detail and enjoy cleaning.

HB: Place a small display advertisement in the business to business and residential phone book directory under janitorial services. Get your first account by estimating the time and materials needed as tightly as possible while yielding a small profit. Let you first account know you are trying to build up customers and any referrals would be greatly appreciated. Almost all businesses will require you to be bonded to work there when everyone else is gone. Call a business insurance broker for a free quote over the phone.

Start Your Business with Very Little Money

P: Be competitive as businesses are trying to cut back on everything they can right now. If you have no employees, your prices can be much lower than your competition as you will not have to pay workers compensation, bonding insurance per employee and payroll taxes.

OPE: Cost of basic cleaning supplies that can be bought in bulk at warehouse stores.

MI: Have a signature type of service that includes anything you like. For example, water indoor potted plants; vacuum a unique pattern on the floor, use a certain air freshener spray scent, leave fresh (inexpensive) flowers in the ladies rest room, etc.

Lawn Service

W: Mowing, edging and manicuring lawns. Trimming trees and bushes as needed.

SN: Small engine service and repair experience, or willing to learn. Be able to work quickly and efficiently in a neat manner.

HB: Preferably, you already have most or all of the needed equipment. Speaking perfect English is a huge asset as people usually have a hard time communicating with most lawn care workers. Focus all of your attention to one or two neighborhoods. Count how many houses are in one neighborhood. If you had fifty houses, it would be a guaranteed full time income and no need to drive all over to perform your service. Pass out business cards and talk to home owners over and over until somebody gives you an opportunity. Make sure their lawn is the best in the neighborhood. Make up a flyer pointing out that you are doing the lawn at 123 Maple Street for $50 a month. They can have the same quality of service for the same price. Keep leaving business cards with a flyer all over that street. Soon, you will muscle out the less hungry competition.

By speaking English proficiently, customers will be eager to ask you to perform additional work, such as hauling away junk, repairing sprinklers, planting new shrubbery and lawns. Also, you can offer an annual lawn feeding, weeding and aeration for an additional charge.

P: The service charges are based on what level of service you plan to perform in what kind of area. More affluent neighborhoods will want more service and attention to detail. The difference will mean only having as low as ten to twenty affluent customers compared to about fifty for a middle class neighborhood. If you plan on earning $750 to $1000 a week; add what the fuel and equipment maintenance will cost for full time work and divide it by the type or combination of types of customers you are focusing on.

OPE: As stated before, hopefully you already have most or all of the needed equipment. The only start up cost should be the printing of your business cards, invoices and flyers.

MI: Secure at least <u>one</u> commercial account like a gas station, business center, shopping center, etc. Even if they will not be very profitable due to the nature of doing work for commercial operations, they will provide some income while establishing your residential (more profitable) customers.

Office Mover
W: Moving office furniture and cubicles from one building to another. Moving offices also includes managing the disconnecting and reconnecting of power and phone lines for each cubicle/ work area.

SN: Training from an existing company is almost required. There are tricks and efficiencies that can only be learned from experience.

HB: Once you get trained from an existing company; place an ad in the business to business directory phone book. Pass out cards to commercial real estate agents as they will be assisting different companies with their new location. Most of your work will come from word of mouth, once you get established. To get started, everything can be rented like specialized dollies, plenty of moving pads and trucks.

There is plenty of steady work in this industry. The pay is excellent as expenses are mostly for fuel and maintenance on your truck, once you have all of your own equipment.

Start Your Business with Very Little Money

P: Bid $25-35 per man hour. Realize that you will almost certainly under bid at first, but after a few mistakes you will be more precise at estimating.

OPE: All of the equipment you need, can be rented at first.

MI: Large office buildings have their own on site management team. Make connections with as many inside people of different buildings as possible for information on new company move ins' and move out's.

Pallet Recycling

W: Pallets are needed by companies shipping items and truck drivers coming to a business that require them to furnish their own. Old, broken pallets can be obtained for free outside shipping companies at the dumpster or by asking for their damaged ones inside. You repair the mildly broken ones and disassemble others to use parts to build fresh pallets.

SN: Wood working skills, have a truck and a place to store completed pallets.

HB: Visit local trucking and shipping companies to locate free pallets and/ or make arrangements to sell pallets to them. If the demand is far greater than the pallets you can recover, build them from scratch. Templates for standard cuts can be made. Lumber, saw and a nail gun is needed. Always have 22 pallets ready to go and be prepared to deliver them at a moments notice. A truck driver typically needs that exact number for their trailer.

If you learn of a shipping company that requires truckers to have their own pallets, be sure they have plenty of your business cards and notify them that you will always be available to deliver the pallets at a moments notice. The shipping company will be glad to as they want their products shipped immediately and the trucker will appreciate it as he will not have to search for them on his own.

P: Clean pallets can be bought from truckers and salvagers for $7-10 and resold back to truckers and shipping companies for $10-15. Recycling broken ones will cost $2-5 to repair. Check your area for local pricing.

Start Your Business with Very Little Money

OPE: No start up costs if you already have the wood working tools and repair broken, abandoned pallets.

MI: Call every national trucking company headquarters and ask to be a vendor for your area. They will send you the information. If accepted, the trucking companies will send you a check in a week or two every time you provide pallets to a driver.

Parking Lot Re-striping
W: Commercial businesses need fresh parking lot paint re-striping when the old lines become faded.

SN: Painting experience and excellent mathematical and measuring skills to determine locations of markings.

HB: Purchase a commercial paint strip machine from an internet search or a commercial paint store. Advertise in the Business to business phone books in many areas around your home.. Talk to every commercial property owner that has worn out paint on their parking lot. Contact asphalt contractors. Some will have their own painters; others will refer you, once they know you conduct business professionally and perform the work to their standards. Expect to travel as this is a specialized business.

P: Contact your competitors to find out your best pricing strategy. Most likely, you can charge $50 an hour plus paint.

OPE: A new paint striping machine (used if you can locate one) and a few gallons of reflective white paint.

MI: Have at least one account from a property management company in charge of multiple shopping and business centers. They will grind you to get your lowest prices but will provide a lot of steady work.

Party D.J.
W: Provide music and structure the entertainment for clubs, bars, wedding receptions, birthday parties (kids and adults), anniversary

celebrations, retirement parties, engagement parties, new years, Halloween, Christmas and Fourth of July parties.

SN: Know and have a wide range of music appropriate for different groups of people. Be able to take control when speaking to a group of loud partiers. Have an outgoing, friendly personality.

HB: Create a catalog of music for each type of party and crowd. Have a menu and a process readily prepared to conduct each type of party. When customers discuss their party with you, you can adjust your plan to fit their needs. Be prepared to work at a moments notice as some D.J.'s will flake at the last minute.

Advertise in the business services directory phone book describing the various types of parties you specialize in. Make connections with party planners, wedding planners, and bakeries (there's almost always a cake involved right?). Give your card to every existing D.J. as a fill in, in case they can't make an engagement. Expect to work most weekends and nights.

P: Depending on the type of party; a child's birthday party may only be a couple of hours and pay $100. An all night adult party can pay up to $500 plus tips, if you are in charge of conducting the event too.

OPE: You should already have most of your own music catalog. The only real expense is the cost of used sound equipment from the internet or equipment trader magazine.

MI: Find a local bar that has a good sized crowd on weekends but only uses a juke box for entertainment. Offer your services (for free if needed) to hone your skills and accept tips too. Have business cards ready and casually mention several times during the night that you're available for parties, weddings etc.

Party Rental, Kids Bouncers
W: Kids' bouncers are becoming common at weekend and holiday parties and of course, kid's birthday parties. People pay a party rental company to bring a bouncer before the party and return afterwards to disassemble and remove.

SN: Have a truck, a place to store bouncers and be available mostly on weekends and holidays to set up and disassemble party bouncers.

HB: A small full color business services directory phone book listing is almost required for advertising. Party bouncers can be purchased wholesale from an internet search or a business to business phone book. The bouncers need constant maintenance, cleaning and repairs. You should have an area that is convenient to set up and perform those tasks nearby after each rental. Be alert to safety concerns on every rental. Some parents don't realize how kids can bounce out or that children can become bullies at times. The bouncer needs an adult to sign for responsibility for any accidents or incidents. The bouncer should be placed close to the party so many adults can keep an eye on the kids. The bouncer needs to be installed in a safe place, away from traffic or hazards. This business is easily expandable by offering tables and chairs to rent to the same customers. People in a party mood aren't pinching pennies.

P: Rentals are around $200 and up to $500 for the most elaborate, newer models. A new bouncer costs $2500 to $7500. Fifteen to twenty rental days will pay for itself. Every rental afterwards is almost pure profit.

OPE: Many bouncer rentals are an after thought by parents giving a party or picnic when family and friends are expected to bring their children. When they buy alcohol for the adults at the liquor store, they'll think "what about the kids entertainment while the adults talk?" Make an agreement with local liquor stores to give out your business cards. Hand write or stamp on the back, "ten percent discount for all XXXX Liquor Store customers". Take that discount marked business card and give the customer a couple of unmarked business cards, one to pass out and the other to keep. Pay the local liquor store owner ten or twenty dollars cash for each referral. Afterwards, he will <u>definitely</u> remember to give out your card to every single customer who buys liquor for a party.

Pet Grooming, Mobile Service
W: Pet washing and clipping in front of the customers house in a van or cargo trailer with windows installed.

Start Your Business with Very Little Money

SN: Experience with pet grooming.

HB: This is a fairly new business that seems to be doing well. As you know, some people treat their pets as a true family member. They want the best for their pet at any cost. This service is convenient and quicker for the customer. Your cost is much less than paying rent for a store front location.

A cargo trailer (preferably a used concessionaire type) can be outfitted with an electric 5 gallon water heater ($250 plus plumbing) that is fed by the customers' water hose, powered by a portable generator ($500 new), that also supplies electricity for your clippers, dryer and vacuum. A groomers table and a large wash basin can be placed in front of the window, bolted to the floor. The drain for the wash basin can be connected to another hose that can be placed on their lawn, Check with the city as they may require you to dump the water in an approved drain; if required, install a sanitary waste tank underneath the trailer and dispose the waste water later in an appropriate drain.

It would benefit you greatly to have an advertising graphics on the side of your trailer. At the very least, have professional lettering on all four sides of the trailer. Of course, advertise in the phone book too.

P: Mobile groomers can charge anywhere from $50- 150, depending on the time and service.

OPE: A used concessionaires 12' trailer should cost less than $2500, outfitting it yourself will cost about $1500; and paying someone to install the equipment for you will probably cost another $1500.

MI: Ask your friends if you can groom their pets for a major discount on Saturday's or early evenings in nice neighborhoods when most of the neighbors are home They will see you through the window grooming pets and ask you to groom theirs too.

Photographer
W: a photographer takes wedding pictures, portraits and event photos.

SN: Must know or learn every aspect of lighting and photography. Some community colleges offer a semester course.

HB: Place a small advertisement in local magazines aimed at the wealthier families in your area. Go to popular holiday events in your area and take lots of pictures. Find a pilot who would be interested in flying you over events to take photos. Post them on your newly created website with on offer to sell large prints. Be sure to carry a handful of cards. You will be asked at events how someone could get pictures. Be sure to include the date and place, digitally added, to event photographs. Also, anytime there is an incident or accident, take pictures and call the newspaper and television studios with an offer to sell. A business services directory advertisement will bring you some portrait work for individuals and families.

P: Compare with other photographers prices. Talk to other local photographers to find out what the newspaper and television stations will pay for incidents, prior to learning afterwards.

OPE: High quality photography equipment, used in good condition.

MI: Be creative. Digitally enhanced photos are so artistic; they can be framed as art work. Consider purchasing photography software and learn to master it. Buy some nice quality frames and you could sell the pictures at a swap meet, on EBay or in restaurants. Restaurants will sometimes allow you to hang pictures with your business card and for sale price. They get a steady stream of fresh artwork to liven up their décor for free.

Plant Nursery, Shaped Bushes

W: Grow bushes and train into fun designs and animal shapes.

SN: Be artistic; enjoy working outdoors with plants, not afraid to fail at creativity. Have a yard or area to grow about 100 or more plants at a time, with each one growing to a 2-3' radius.

HB: Many people would like to purchase fun shaped bushes. You probably have already seen the starter plants with pre formed wire mesh animal shapes. There is a market for more mature, trained plants that the

Start Your Business with Very Little Money

homeowner can just touch up as needed, but not have to wait for the plant to fill in the wire mesh. They take time to form and train. Starter plants are basically free when grown from cloning. Cloning is easy after studying different methods from the internet and trying a few times. Training and shaping takes trial and error practice.

Purchase a growing tray for up to 30 plants at a time. Out of thirty, you should get about 25 healthy starter plants. Place those in one gallon containers. Start to look and study your plants and imagine what shape each one is trying to form naturally and begin to trim and train accordingly. Keep producing starter plants. When the plants in the one gallon buckets appear to become crowded, start to transplant each one into a three gallon bucket and get them ready to sell. Very soon, you will have created a pipeline of plants ready to sell every week. Trimming and training should only take a few hours a week along with watering. You will have created an income from very little time and effort.

With your creativity, you can create some really interesting shaped bushes in every form you can imagine. Make each bush interesting and unique to get the highest price from your nursery. Take your plants to the swap meet and sell directly to homeowners.

P: $35-100 per plant, depending on the interesting, artistic shape and size of each plant.

OPE: Less than $200 for used plant containers, used bush trimmer, growing tray, potting soil and nutrients.

MI: Post pictures and sell on EBay and craigslist.org. You may sell many more plants at better prices by shipping them all over the country.

Pool Cleaning Route

W: Clean residential pools on a weekly basis. Repair their equipment and acid wash pools when needed for an extra charge.

SN: Know how to clean pools, or be willing to learn.

HB: Pool routes are offered for sale all the time in the newspaper. Purchasing a route usually includes training on the basics. Many sellers

Start Your Business with Very Little Money

will accept monthly payments with a down payment. If you prefer to start your own route, word of mouth will be the most effective. Canvas every home you know that has a pool. Contact homeowner associations to bid on their pool contract. Try a penny saver advertisement with minimum wording for several weeks. Once established, expect steady pay and hours with the possibility of selling the route for a nice profit later.

P: Depending on what area and what the pool size is, expect to receive $50-150 per pool per month.

OPE: The cost of purchasing the route (if so) plus chemicals and cleaning equipment.

MI: With so many foreclosures, real estate agents are usually in charge of maintaining homes until they are sold. Many cities and counties require upkeep or draining as pools are mosquito ridden after being neglected. With effort, real estate agents who are in charge of these homes can be located.

Process Server

W: Attorneys and plaintiffs must use a legal process server to hand official court documents to people being served. A process server signs a legal document that the papers were served.

SN: Detective like skills, patience and persistence.

HB: Check your state on the requirements to become a legal process server. Find a local magazine that serves the legal community for your area. Place a small advertisement. There is usually reasonable time to serve someone. Many times, the recipient is expecting to be served and will avoid you at all cost. Being successful requires strategy and quick thinking. Word of mouth about your persistence and success will bring you more business from other attorneys.
The job is easy but doesn't pay very well.

P: Expect about $50-75 for each person being served. One person may require 15 minutes to serve while another person may take days.

OPE: The fees (along with the paperwork) paid to your sate to become legal.

MI: Some attorneys will gladly take a major discount for their needs in exchange for referring you to their friends and associates, which pay regular prices.

Produce or Flower Distributor

W: Every major city has a produce and flower district. A distributor makes agreements with wholesalers to sell their products to local flower shops or small grocery/ convenience stores. A distributor purchases (or takes on consignment) products that he thinks the small stores will or could purchase that day or week.

SN: Be an excellent negotiator, have sales experience, be willing to work early mornings and drive to a major city to pick up your products each day.

HB: Find the wholesale markets in larger cities. If you are between two cities, check them both. Talk to the wholesalers about being a distributor. Businesses are based on relationships. Be at your best and realize that several trips and attempts may be needed to establish some trust for both the people you sell to (retailers) and the people you buy from (wholesalers).

Consider what kinds of businesses you want to service and what they need. Specialize in one segment of the industry, while providing the usual basics to other businesses. For example; if you choose to be a produce distributor, you could specialize in Japanese and/or Chinese restaurants. Remember that schools, corporate cafeterias and golf courses need produce for their kitchens too.

If you choose to be a flower distributor; you could specialize in servicing florists near, or in hospitals. Being a flower distributor is a bit tricky. The demand is "off the charts" high for certain holidays and a little stale otherwise. Reliability and fair pricing though out the year will make you their supplier for peak times too.

Start Your Business with Very Little Money

Have a 24 hour fax available for your customers to be able to order products for delivery the next day. They can fax you whenever they realize they need something immediately and will not have to rely on their memory or worry about missing you when you deliver. Each morning, you check the fax machine and add those items to your orders.

When visiting your prospective customers, realize that you are providing an additional supplier for their needs. Healthy competition! You shouldn't feel like you're approaching the customer with "your hat in your hands". Visit your prospective customer during slow times and ask to see the manager. Many employees are trained to head off salesmen at the door. If you're turned away, be polite and hand the card to that employee anyway and come back at a different time and day the next week. When speaking to a manager/ owner; be straight up and honest that you're new to this business and will guarantee the absolute lowest prices and best service if he will trust you with the next order. Even if you lose money by servicing just one customer, the ball will be rolling (and your confidence will grow!).

Ask to be paid in cash at the time of delivery, as it is standard practice. Be aware that any customer who asks to pay you later on the first order is a huge red flag. If they pay by check, run it to the bank immediately. After awhile, trust is established on both sides. Big chain florist/ restaurants should be avoided in the beginning. They pay monthly and you may not have the working capital to keep your business running if the checks are delayed, and checks never seem to come when you *really* need them.

P: Be sure you are providing the lowest prices, especially when just starting out. Ask managers to show you any invoice from a competitor and you'll beat their price by 10%!

OPE: Start up cost is printing your business cards and invoices and your gas and time to build a route. You need a van or truck to carry your product. During hot months, you will need to get a portable air conditioner or purchase ice to keep everything cold while making your deliveries.

MI: Being a distributor has many growth opportunities. After studying your customers, you will find other types of products that are easy to

94

carry and sell for a good profit. For example: Buy in bulk, ribbons and accessories, and always carry a variety to offer them to florist when they're purchasing your flowers.

Recycling

W: Many items are recyclable that can be sold for cash.

SN: Learn different markets and pricing on a variety of items. Accurately judge the weight by sight of materials.

HB: Most people know about cardboard, paper, metals and returnable bottles. How about recycling car batteries, carpet padding and plastics? I *know* there's much more recycling materials than I've listed here. As of this writing, the price of recycled materials has plunged dramatically and is starting to rise and stabilize. Many states have redemption values for containers that still make worth recycling feasible. This is the time to become established when most people are getting out of the business.

Recycling centers are notorious for short changing customers. Talk to anyone who recycles on a regular basis and they will usually tell you that they have found the center that <u>rips them off less</u> than the other companies! Pathetic.

Take the recycling to the businesses that have items to recycle. Plumbing companies have old brass and copper. Carpet companies have old padding. Window replacement companies have aluminum. Small wrecking yards have old batteries. You purchase the items fairly from companies with a small charge added to pick up and process the materials. Resell the items at much larger quantities for top dollar from the most reputable company you can find. A buyer would hesitate to short change you, since you can take your business elsewhere tomorrow, and he knows that *you know the actual weight and value* of each load, before he even weighs it. It takes much less effort to purchase your scrap because you know the routine and you bring him more than ten of his average customers.

Start Your Business with Very Little Money

Sometimes, you can follow recycling centers trucks when they leave to find out where *they* are taking the materials. Eventually, you can cut out the middle man and accumulate the required minimum load for the best paying buyer.

P: Buy low, sell high! Be consistently fair in weighing your customers scrap, just pay a little less per pound, they will respect you for it and refuse to do much of any business with anyone else.

OPE: $3-500 for your first purchases of scrap.

MI: Contact large business centers to get permission to set up recycling bins. Once a week or more, go around and take the returnable aluminum, plastic bottles and wipe down the bins. Have a maintenance man verify the weight each time and send them a check. They get additional income for no additional effort.

Roadside Automobile Service

W: Changing or repairing tires, jump starting or replacing batteries, opening locked vehicles and bringing antifreeze to customers in need. **SN:** Have auto repair experience and a truck with a compressor. Learn how to open vehicles with a Slim Jim, (or do not provide service for opening locked vehicles).

HB: The basic equipment is a floor jack, star wrench, can gasoline, can of diesel, extra long jumper cables, gallon of antifreeze, a few batteries with different posts, and possibly a Slim Jim kit.

Advertise in the business services directory in several listings: Batteries, tires, roadside services, locksmiths and auto repair. Make sure your company has "roadside service" in the name. People will find your company one way or another. In order to keep advertising costs down, consider just listing your business name under each section, rather than purchasing display ads.

Have your truck lettered on all sides. Many times, you will be "waived down" as you drive (slowly) by people with flat tires on the road.

Start Your Business with Very Little Money

The Automobile club, All State Insurance, State Farm and many others offer roadside assistance in their policies. They do not pay very well, but the volume of calls they give you to service makes it very profitable. Call or do an internet search on how to become a vendor for each company. With a city business license, insurance, uniforms and proper equipment, you may be pleasantly surprised of how easy it is to become a vendor!

P: $50-75 per call, half or less working for a major insurance company.

OPE: Lettering your truck $300-500, equipment purchased used $300, printing
Invoices and cards $200-300.

MI: Talk to auto repair shops and give them your card. Many times, a customer will call them in desperation. The mechanics are sometimes not interested in having to tow the vehicle for a dead battery or flat tire and would rather have you take the problem off of them. In exchange you can also refer all the customers who have more serious engine problems to that   mechanic.

Screen Repair Service

W: Replace screens on windows and doors for home and businesses. Repair and/or replace screen doors.

SN: Practice replacing screens on friends and families homes. Learn by trial and error. Be somewhat mechanically inclined.

HB: To start, almost everything you could possibly need can be found at a heavy duty hardware store or a home improvement store. After establishing your business, full screen rolls and needed hardware can be found in the B2B directory and purchased in bulk.

A small utility trailer is usually used with a home made table for the top, placed about waist high for a working area. Rolls of different colored screens and extra hardware are placed inside, under the table in built in cabinets. A ladder and drop cloths make the job easier and cleaner.

This is a fairly easy job that can be a little dusty sometimes. Always carry a few different quality grades of screen doors to offer customers. Establish one or more commercial customers for steady, but lesser paying work. Advertise in the local business directory phone books however far you are willing to travel. To get the ball rolling, place a small ad in the penny saver and local newspaper and run the ad continuously, even when you get little or no response. People have a habit of collecting information or looking through old issues and will call you, sometimes, a year or more later.

P: Depending on your competition, one average screen replacement for $75, and several at the same property for $25-35 each. New screen doors: $100 plus 150% of your cost of the door.

OPE: Purchase several yards of different types of screens and have some hardware ($200-500). A used utility trailer can be purchased and fitted for $500- $1500, but you can wait on that if you're starting with as little money as possible. If so, bring a couple of sheets of plywood and saw horses to use as a table.

MI: Volunteer to replace the screens for free at churches, community service location, etc., anywhere that a lot of people congregate and has some kind of newsletter or bulletin. Make a clear agreement with the leader that their members be made aware that you provided this service at no cost, and how members can contact your business directly in their bulletin or newsletter.

Sliding Glass Door Repair
W: Repair or replace rollers and locks on big sliding glass doors.

SN: Trial and error. Most big glass doors SHOULD BE SHATTER PROOF, if not; the glass could kill or seriously hurt you if it falls down. You should have the strength to handle a heavy, breakable, possibly dangerous and large door.

HB: Most parts can be found at a good hardware store. If they don't carry something, they can usually order the part and provide it within a

Start Your Business with Very Little Money

reasonable amount of time. The work is simple, especially after you've repaired several different kinds. Your tools and materials can be put in the trunk of a compact car. Each door should take less than an hour to repair, provided you have the correct parts on hand.

This is a highly specialized job. Advertise in every publication, far and wide, with the minimum required description for listing your business.

P: $99 is a fair price since materials will cost you less than $5-10 and it takes less than an hour from start to finish.

OPE: Less than $200 to have the parts that you *could* possibly need.

MI: Mobile home parks and retirement communities are great places to get business. Give a huge discount and still make a ton of money. Ask the management to agree on having a semi annual service announcement for all residents only on certain dates of the year. For example: "60% off to Sunshine retirement community residents who schedule service on the first Friday in May and November". You eliminate the driving time between jobs and usually all the units or homes are the same exact door, so all the parts are the same. After the first two repairs, you soon get into a rhythm that makes each repair take half the usual time. It will feel like you're just picking up a check for very little work at each place.

Small Appliance Repair, Store Front

W: Repair small appliances at your store front location.

SN: Be mechanically inclined, willing to learn, work on small mechanical items.

HB: There is huge money in small appliance repair from a store front location. People will see your store and eventually bring their vacuum cleaner, toaster, blender, electric razor, radio, clock, coffee maker, espresso machine, phone, etc. An old neighbor of mine had this business and owned the biggest house on the block and always drove the newest Mercedes available. I brought an expensive vacuum to be repaired and he wanted to charge me 2/3^{rds} the value of purchasing another one brand new. I fixed it myself for almost nothing (because I am mechanically inclined and curios enough to try).

To learn, go to the local Salvation Army or goodwill head quarters and tell them you are trying to learn how to repair small appliances. Ask them to give you (or sell you at a major discount) their broken appliances from donations. Figure out each one by doing an internet search on the manufacturers' web site, purchasing repair manuals for small appliances or trial and error. You can always try to find employment at a repair shop away from where you plan to open one.

A store is nothing more than a customer area with a carpeted counter top separating the customer entrance from the back, where repairs are made. Consider having new vacuums for sale in the customer area. You want the highest visibility with the cheapest rent, smallest space available. Shopping centers usually have a big sign listing all the businesses in the plaza.

Place a small ad in the business services directory phone book with your days and hours of operation listed. Many people will just come in without calling first. A neighborhood flyer with a refrigerator magnet attached to each one could be passed out to every home in the area.

P: Some people grow an emotional attachment to their property. When estimating a repair, allow the customer an opportunity to give you their approval, even if it doesn't make monetary sense to make the repair. Also, keep in mind that once in a while, an attempted repair becomes a nightmare and YOU have to provide the parts and labor to finish the job. Be sure to <u>estimate each job on a "worse case scenario" basis</u>. If the repair turns out to be quick and easy, either discount the bill when they come to pick it up, or use the extra funds as a "warranty", in case they bring the appliance back later with the same problem and additional repairs are required.

OPE: A lease on a store front location is the biggest expense. Be sure to have at least a years worth of monthly payments set aside.

MI: Business will be slow. Offer your services to thrift shops, goodwill, salvation army etc. at a *major* discount. Accumulate broken appliances to repair wherever you find them and sell the items in your store and at a swap meet once a month.

Sprinkler Repairs for Lawns

W: Repair and replace sprinkler heads, broken pipes, manifolds, automatic systems, etc.

SN: Experience, or willing to learn everything about watering systems for lawns. This job sometimes gets a bit muddy.

HB: Get hired with a gardening service that repairs their customers' sprinklers. Some gardeners do not provide this service; take notes on companies that do or do not and offer your service to those that don't after you get fully trained. There are complications to repairing sprinkler systems. Many systems were installed by home owners and laborers who were not professional. A thorough assessment is required on every job. If you plan on learning as you go, be prepared to "walk away" from some jobs if you get in too deep. You will have some frustrated customers who will <u>not pay</u> you for your hours of efforts.

Advertise in the newspaper home repairs section on Thursday through Sunday only. Newspapers have their highest circulation on those days. You get a better rate and are advertising only when your customers will most likely be using your service. As stated before, give a card to every gardening service you see as you drive around. Give them 10% of every job they refer to you. Most gardeners have a full route and don't have the time to spend on repairing customers sprinklers. Also, by referring work to you, they separate themselves from the job and limit the customer from trying to get them to make repairs for free.

P: Easily charge $30-40 per home or hour. Since you are specialized in this one area, you will be fast and efficient and be able to offer more fine tuning for an additional charge.

OPE: Most sprinkler equipment is inexpensive. PVC pipe and fittings are typically used and cost very little. About $100 in start up supplies should be more than enough to repair just about anything.

MI: Offer an annual maintenance agreement to every customer. Ask that it is paid in advance. Size up their system and estimate what three average repairs would cost for your agreement. In the agreement, they can call you anytime during the year and repairs are covered. You will also check the system every month and make adjustments as needed.

Swap Meet and EBay Sales

W: Selling items at a local swap meet and/or on the internet.

SN: Specialize in one type of product and have knowledge of several others.

HB: Selling products at swap meets and online is hardly profitable, unless: you sell large quantities of product or you pay almost nothing for the items in the first place (see: Hauling Service).

Bulk items can be purchased from Good Will industries, The Salvation Army, self storage auctions, estate sales, the first or last half hour of almost any garage sale, city, county and government auctions, and store closeouts. The bulk items are purchased for about ten to fifteen cents for every dollar you can sell it for.

Concentrate your efforts on one type of specialty and resell the rest in bulk to other sellers as needed. An example would be selling kid's toys, clothing, artwork, kitchen items, packaged food, cleaning items, etc. Anyone looking for your specialty will definitely stop to check out your merchandise. If there are a wide variety of items, it looks messy and is easier for the shoppers to just pass by, even though you may have exactly what they're looking for.

You can obtain new items for sale by becoming a distributor for a manufacturer, purchasing through an existing manufacturers distributor or purchasing returns/ damaged items from manufacturers and companies directly. You can also buy large quantities of one type of item from overseas manufacturers, like China (See: Importer).

P: New products are usually sold for double what it cost you, it's called key stoning. Selling at swap meets and the internet costs much less than having a sales force and a store to maintain, so the ratio is lower, 30-60%

Start Your Business with Very Little Money

over your costs, depending on how long it takes to sell your average item. Used products are sold at 40-70% of their original value, depending on quality and type of item.

OPE: $200- 1000 for purchasing your first items in bulk for used merchandise.
New items are 3 to 5 times that for bulk purchases.

MI: Craigslist.org is another way to sell items. It costs you nothing to advertise.

Trucking Broker

W: Independent truckers (not working for a major company) find themself in areas without loads to take back home. They can double their profit if they find a paying load back the other way. A trucking broker serves both the trucker and the local companies who occasionally need a truckload shipped. You charge 10-30% of each load, the checks are sent directly to you in your name. You immediately deposit the truckers' money into his bank account once funds have cleared your bank.

SN: A cool head, negotiating skills, networking and phone skills.

HB: Get hired as a dispatcher at a local trucking company. Have a C.B. radio and get to know truckers coming into and out of your area. Do plenty of research on what and when different companies are looking to ship. Build up two separate information notebooks, one for truckers and the other for local companies. Soon, you will be able to predict with precision which trucker should go where and when. Check your state for laws about becoming a trucking broker, you may need to get bonded and/ or licensed.

After working for a trucking company for a short while, you will notice that they get tired and irritable after being on the road awhile. A small issue can put them on edge sometimes. They will know that they can count on you to smooth problems over and get them turned around and headed home ASAP!

OPE: A used CB radio will cost less than $200, and printing business cards and invoices.

MI: Make contact and begin to build relationships with ALL truckers and trucking companies, regardless of size. If you have a lock on the local shipping needs for your area, even the big guys will sometimes go through you to get a paying load to their next destination.

Wall Paper Removal Service

W: If you have ever tried to remove professionally installed wall paper yourself, you know why this service exists.

SN: Experience through working for someone or researching removal products and techniques through paint stores and manufacturers and practicing on your home. Be presentable; dress appropriately, speak politely and be groomed. Your main type of customer definitely cares about who they have in their home.

HB: The wealthy and upper middle class continue to remodel, even when what they have looks fine already. Get the skills to confidentially handle any paper removal job. Even if you have to work for free (for a week) with a distant competitor, there are many tricks to the trade.

Contact every single painter (as far as you dare to work) to be a sub-contractor on any of their projects. Advertise in the B2B, business services directory phone book and upscale local home improvement magazines. This is a specialized service; so small, inexpensive ads will work just as well as the big expensive ads.

Be prepared to travel some distances for work. Again, this is highly specialized. Everything you will need fits in a compact car.

P: $30-45 an hour flat rate. Do you really know how many layers of wall paper are underneath the one you see? If you damage anything, expect to pay for it. Be firm in your prices or get them to sign for exceptions if there are more layers; and, *who* is required to patch any holes in the wall afterwards.

OPE: Less than $100 plus advertising, if needed.

MI: Once established, you will get most of your business through word

Start Your Business with Very Little Money
of mouth. Consider it a major blessing if you get a chance to bid on a project with a high strung talkative home owner that's dressed in fashionable clothing. Bid low on your hourly rate, be fast, clean, professional and super-super thorough in your work. She is well connected to others like her that has money to spend. Do a great job and she will refer you over and over. When you work for her friends, they will do the same. By eliminating the need for advertising, your profit is increased by 10-20%.

For Businesses Not Included Here.....

Anything legal and morally acceptable is fair game! Pursue what you love and find a way to make money doing it. Read through each business description (again) for ideas and examples on how to start your business.

The Last Word

Whatever you do in life to provide you and your family an income, enjoy your work. If you are in a job just to survive, at least have a plan and take steps, even small steps, to get to where you want to be in life. The older you get, the quicker time seems to fly by. Your goals and plans need a set timeline for each step along the way. Otherwise, life will pass you by. Take a moment to consider what your thoughts will be when you are 80 or 90 years old. Will you be filled with regrets (shoulda' coulda' woulda'), or fond memories?

Your questions and comments are appreciated:
Rod Condit
P.O. Box 412
Placentia, Ca 92871
powerrod@sbcglobal.net

www.ingramcontent.com/pod-product-compliance
Lightning Source LLC
Chambersburg PA
CBHW072038190526
45165CB00018B/1083